A WINDOW TO THE RUSSIAN SOUL

Ancient Folk Wisdom for Modern Life

NICHOLAS KOTAR

WAYSTONE
PRESS

FOREWORD

We live in a strange time. We put much of our faith in science, even as more and more of the truths we commonly associate with "irrefutable fact" come under scrutiny. The lack of repeatability of many experiments is a modern science's open secret, and much of what can be verified, it turns out, often confirms what history, literature, and religion have already taught us.

Thus, we are learning about the power of reading to effect meaningful change on the level of brain chemistry. But anyone who studies the classics would be able to tell you as much. Research into psychology has shown that habit change is most effective when performed as a change of identity. Religion has maintained that same truth for millennia.

And so, many people are turning to the past for comforting wisdom to inform the future.

This book is an exploration of the rich culture of the Russian peasant. Reading it in light of modern life, you can't help but be astounded at how much wisdom the peasant gathered through centuries and millennia of passed time and experience.

Unlike the two other books in the *Worldbuilding* series

(How to Survive a Russian Fairy Tale and *Heroes for All Time)*, this book is unified less by subject matter and more by a specific point of view toward the past. Much of this material is research for my novels that I shared on my author blog on nicholaskotar.com. It is my hope that if you read this book in conjunction with my *Raven Son* series, your enjoyment of my fantasies will be enriched and deepened.

-Nicholas Kotar

Author of the *Raven Son* epic fantasy series inspired by Russian fairy tales

CHAPTER 1
WINDOWS: EYES INTO THE
SOUL?

aturally, a book with such a pompous title *should*
begin with a chapter on windows. But this is not, I
dare say, the chapter you might expect.

Apparently, some Russians are willing to ascribe great
symbolism to their windows. For the most part, I agree that
windows can be symbolic. But as with many things Russian,
there are some who take such symbolism to an almost comical
extreme. The following is an example—my translation of an
article that insists that Russian windows are a sign of cultural
superiority over the West, and over England specifically.

As I said, I like the idea of "the symbolism of windows,"
but in no way am I advocating the position of the author of
this article. I'm including it here, because it's curious reading,
and in many ways it offers, in spite of itself, a window into the
Russian soul by presenting the Russian tendency to exaggerate,
to find profound meaning in the mundane, and to seek proof
of cultural superiority over the West at every possible
juncture.

WINDOWS: THE EYES OF THE SOUL?

In what ways do Russians differ from, say, the English? Well, there are many. Language, anthropology, culture. But there's a key difference not often mentioned—a difference of windows. Would you believe that something so trivial could say so much about two very different nations?

In Russian, the word "window" (*okno*) comes from the word "eye" (*oko*). In other words, the window is a kind of visual sense organ of the house. The English word "window" is connected with the idea of "wind". This suggests that the English window is primarily a source of fresh air. That is, the visual aspect is lost. Basically, if the Russian window is an eye, the English window is a nose.

THE ENGLISH WINDOW

At least, it was a nose until the Puritans came along. With the coming to power of the Puritans in England, the English window also became an eye. But not the eye of the house. Instead, it became the eye of society on those in the house. It is well known that Puritans liked the idea of transparency (completely) in one's private life. In fact, it was forbidden to put shutters on windows! Any honorable Puritan, in an upsurge of righteous suspiciousness, should be afforded the opportunity to check if his brother in Christ was living properly.

The English barely managed to get rid of the Puritans, sending them off "over the pond," and soon English windows once again got shuttered. Interestingly, though, the habit was a hard one to break. In some villages in Scotland, it's still considered bad form to shutter your windows. And in formerly Puritan Amsterdam and Lutheran Stockholm, until very recently, there were strict prohibitions on shutters.

The Puritan spirit of watchfulness over others did have its

influence on today's English political tradition. The roots of liberal ideology—the transparency of citizens, an "open" society, all kinds of "watchdog" organizations that do everything from monitoring elections to ostracizing entire countries—all this comes from the habit of looking into others' windows.

THE RUSSIAN WINDOW

Now, back to the traditional Russian window. The interior of the Russian house symbolized the inner world of the human being. It was considered almost a blasphemy to peek into this inner world without invitation. After all, the role of "watcher" was more than ably managed by the icons, which mobilized people to live righteously far better than the peeking eyes of their neighbors.

The doors of a Russian village house were always open for visitors. This, in the mind of the peasant, was connected with the Biblical story of Abraham's hospitality. This is also why, traditionally, the Russian hut always had three windows facing the street.

Russia windows were not there to peek in, but rather to gaze outward onto the world created by God. In other words, windows, in the Russian tradition, are the "eyes" of the people living in the house, not the eyes of society looking in.

CHAPTER 2
THE LOST WORLD OF THE VILLAGE CRADLE

N ew parents know, as no one else, that choosing a bed for their first child is a decision fraught with significance. That being said, more often than not, the choice of cradle will most likely be determined by cost or by loyalty to brand.

But if we look back at the history of village cradles in Russia, we can't help but be struck by the richness of meaning and symbolism of that microcosm. But instead of merely marveling at the past, perhaps there is something in these traditions we can incorporate in our own choices of cradles for our babies.

MAKING THE CRADLE

The cradle was as essential an element of a village home as a table or a stove. Therefore, the making of a family's cradle was entrusted to a real master, always someone with a warm heart as well as golden hands (there's an apt Russian expression meaning "able to do anything he puts his hands to").

Of course, any peasant father could make a simple cradle,

but it was considered important enough for the future of the child to give the job to a master.

The choice of material was not unimportant. There were several options—bast, bulrush, strips of pine, or linden bark. One thing you could never use—aspen. In Russian mythology, aspens were believed to be in league with all sorts of dark powers, and no child would have a happy life if he slept in a cradle made of aspen.

PRACTICAL CONSIDERATIONS

Usually, the cradle was hung in the rear part of the peasant hut, near a small stove used to keep embers warm for the large stove. This stove was lined with thick logs, and a long wooden stake would be nailed into one of these logs. From it, a roll of wire would hang, called a *kachok* ("something that rocks"). The cradle would be attached to this wire by rope. You could rock the cradle using a strap with a hand or with the foot, when the hands were busy.

But there was a kind of science to rocking the cradle. If you pushed a little too hard, it would flip over, and the baby would fall on the floor.

Often this job was given to the older children, especially girls, around their seventh or eighth year. Some of them took great pride in this job, and they became quite talented. They prided themselves on rocking skills that would easily calm a boisterous baby.

THE MICROCOSM OF THE CRADLE

The cradle was a kind of small universe for the baby. It was often decorated in the most fanciful ways. The head had a carving of a sun, and the moon and the stars decorated the feet. Hand-made rattles and toys hung above the baby, as well as colored fabrics, painted wooden spoons, inflated bull bladders with dry peas rattling inside. And, of course, there was always at least one icon and a cross inside the cradle with the baby. The cradle itself was carved all over and painted.

The canopy was an indispensable part of any cradle. It kept annoying insects away and it hid the baby from the evil eyes of others. The most beautiful fabric was chosen for the canopy, and it was further decorated with lace and ribbons. If the family was especially poor, they could use an old sarafan (outer dress) that always looked festive, even if it was old.

The cradle was considered "lucky" if the child grew up healthy inside it—if he didn't get sick often, if he didn't fuss too much, and in general, if he used all of his baby-strength to give joy to his parents by his behavior. Such cradles rarely remained empty for long.

Interestingly, it was considered bad luck to rock an empty cradle, otherwise the future baby would not have pleasant dreams. This old superstition has survived to our days.

When a "lucky" cradle was no longer needed, you couldn't simply throw it out. You needed to carry it into the woods and hang it on a birch branch.

HANGING THE CRADLE

There were many reasons why the cradle must never be placed on the floor. For example, it was believed that angels could better protect a child that was "above the ground." And if he were to lie on the ground, the mice could get in (or, God forbid, the *domovoi*!) That's why all kinds of sharp implements were placed under a hanging cradle—scissors, knives, combs— these protected the baby against evil spirits. Another well-known protector of the baby was the family cat, which, as everyone knows, got along very well with the *domovoi*.

Russian peasants had many interesting ideas about a baby's sleep habits. Many of these ideas were rooted in Russian paganism. For example, a log was sometimes placed next to the baby, along with an incantation: "Sleep as deeply as this log." There's a deeper significance to this action—the log acts as a kind of "double" of the baby. Apparently, if evil spirits decided to harm the baby, they might confuse the baby with the log.

There was also an evil spirit associated with waking babies, called *Budukha* (literally, "one who wakes up"). Parents did everything possible to keep on his good side. Cradles often had spells painted onto their sides. Just to make sure, the parents always left something sweet for *Budukha*. If the baby had trouble sleeping, they might even hang the cradle in a different place, to make room for *Budukha*.

OTHER SUPERSTITIONS

- If the baby still didn't want to fall asleep, the parents carried the cradle out to the porch. They would then ask the Dawn to take away the baby's insomnia.
- You should never pass a cradle over a doorstep.
- You should never leave a cradle alone, because the evil spirits could easily switch your baby with a demon child.
- A child should not be put into a cradle before baptism.

Of course, the best way of making a child fall asleep was the lullaby, which was so effective that sometimes more than the baby fell asleep.

CHAPTER 3
RITUAL LAMENTATION

Russian mothers did not limit their musical talents only to lullabies. Singing, or more specifically, ritual lamentation, was an important part of every phase of life for Russian people. Mothers keened and wailed when their young daughters were married, when people were buried, when a beloved son was recruited into the army. These songs moved the members of the community to share the suffering, and they cleansed the singer from her pain. Such lamentation also ritually "freed" the one being wept over for his or her new life, whatever form it might take.

THE LAMENT OF PARTING: WEDDINGS

The bride began to keen from the moment of her betrothal and didn't stop until the wedding. She cried over the loss of her maiden beauty, her father's house, her former way of life. It was a way to erase the past, to become a blank page, to die and come to life again in a new form—a married woman.

Sometimes, girls were married off without their consent. In those cases, the wailing was more than a symbol. But in any case, no girl could help lament the end of her girlhood and having to leave the nest of her beloved parents.

Every day, the "poor wailer" would go out on her porch and begin to sing loudly, and her friends would lament with her. While she sewed her wedding dress, they would lament without stopping. There was a special lament for the moment when her braid was undone and replaited in two. The braid was a symbol of her "maiden beauty," her youth. Even when the groom would visit with his family, the girls would continue to sing. Even on the way to church, the singing didn't stop.

It was the only way to express her worries about the coming changes. Any such ritual lament indicated a passage into a new phase of life, a rejection of the past, and the acceptance of a strange future.

THE LAMENT OF PARTING: FUNERALS

The widow or orphan wept for their loss, blamed the dead person for abandoning them, for leaving them to fate. The sorrow at such a loss could be so strong that physically, a person could do little more than wail. The sound was symbolic of the soul leaving the body.

Thus, by wailing, the one left alive became like the dead person and symbolically accompanied him on his last journey. The wailer was, as it were, caught between two world—the world of the living and the world of the dead. These songs remembered the past, considered the future (even in some ways becoming a kind of prophecy), and bemoaned the present. Ultimately, they were a way of releasing the soul for its final journey, despite the protest expressed in the wailing.

THE LAMENT OF PARTING: RECRUITMENT

If a husband, son, or brother was called to war, the women expressed their social or political protest through ritual keening or laments. Every time someone left to war, the whole village would take part in the lament. It was also a way to give vent to sorrow, and there were often reasons to sorrow aplenty.

After all, peasants were more often than not impressed into armed service. They would be chained in case of possible flight. They would often be beaten into service. The ritual lament was the only way for the women to express their horror at the way their men were treated, and so these songs are some of the most poignant.

THE PROFESSION OF LAMENTATION

Not everyone was capable of giving expression to a real, living sorrow in a way that was emotional, sincere, and so powerful as to move others to tears. All these elements are necessary if the sorrow is to be overcome and destroyed. The lament is not just crying, it is poetry, the anguish of the soul put into concrete language. In some situations, tears were not even necessary.

Therefore, more often than not, professional wailing women were called to help. They had special mannerisms and ways of singing, and each one was unique. One could sing emotionally, with actual tears, her voice breaking, us though she were about to pass out. But another might sing without any emotion, without tears, using the strong imagery of the songs, the symbolism to move people to sympathetic suffering.

For example, Irina Fedosova, a famous professional lamenter from Olonetsk, was an artist of the lament. She would not even begin to sing until she had interviewed all the friends and relatives about the details of their lives and sorrows. Then she would choose the best information and create poetic images around them.

By lamenting someone else's sorrow, the professional could include in her songs not only the sorrowful present, but intertwine it with the joyful past, and include hints about a possible future. So it wasn't just a cry of the soul, but a conversation between the past and the future, a telling of a story.

No professional wailer ever mentioned her own name as the "artist." She always transformed completely, becoming the person on whose behalf she was lamenting, whether that was a young widow, an orphan, a neighbor, a mother that lost her young child.

IMPROVISATION

The ritual lament is a fascinating mix of artistry and native folk tradition. It is filled with poetic images of nature and scenes from the life of the person being lamented. So every song is unique and impossible to be replicated.

No lament was ever sung the same way twice. Every event had its own special telling and special lamentation. It is, after all, an event rooted in the present moment, having a strict set of rules for the given situation, whether a wedding, a funeral, or recruitment.

Not only the words, but the music was also subject to such improvisation, giving each song its unique stamp, and making each professional wailer a true artist in her own right.

Ultimately, the reason for lamentation is two-fold. It's an expression of powerlessness before fate, injustice, and death. This expression allowed sorrow to reach its full pitch. But the other side of the coin is that through lamentation, joy became possible again. Only after lamenting can the griever find the strength to laugh again. After night, the sun rises again. After winter, spring comes. This is why there is such a mix of joy in sadness in so many Russian folk songs.

CHAPTER 4
FOLK WEDDINGS

Perhaps no event in life is such a rich combination of joy and sorrow as a wedding. Not surprisingly, there were many rituals and folk traditions in old Russia that celebrated both aspects. Here are some of the more fascinating traditions. These are, it must be said, simplifications and generalizations. But some aspect of each of these would have been normal in any peasant village wedding.

THE MATCHMAKING

The process of matchmaking started with the unexpected arrival of the prospective groom with his entire family at the bride's house. It was a chance for both young people to see each other and to be seen. But there's a symbolic moment here as well. The matchmaking was the point of no return, the point at which the bride and groom entered the ritual space of the preparation for the wedding.

From this moment, the bride was severely limited in movement. She should not even leave the house of her parents! If a young girl did leave, it was with her female friends, and even then, only to invite people to the wedding. The bride was also forbidden from doing any housework. It was a kind of death, necessary for her to be reborn as a new person, a member of another family.

THE "VIEWING"

Two or three days after the matchmaking, the groom and his close friends arrived at the house of the bride for the official "viewing" (*smotriny*). The young lady was supposed to show herself off in all her finery, to demonstrate all her abilities. The young man would then do the same. After this, the mother of the groom examined the bride's dowry. All this was, of course, accompanied by songs and ritual lamentation, as mentioned in the previous chapter, most often done by the bride's friends. At this point, the bride could still decide to refuse the groom by simply not coming out for the viewing.

One interesting local practice is the "washing" of the bride. In some regions, in honor of Mother Earth, a young man showed his preference for a bride by drenching her with water. If he drenched her, he had to officially court her. If he didn't go through with it, he would be universally reviled.

One of the early Chronicles describes this rite with a healthy dose of early Christian disapproval:

> Some people sacrifice living people to some kind of god by drowning them. This mad practice continues in some countries. The young people, gathering together, throw a person into the water, and sometimes, by the action of those evil gods, that is, demons, the victims are broken and killed. In other places the victims are only drenched with water, but this is still a sacrifice to that same demon.

THE ENGAGEMENT

This was the event that finalized the agreement between families. No one could refuse to get married after this event. The bride and groom were seated at the table. Various songs were sung to them. The bride said nothing, but she performed the ritual song of lamentation. In some houses, professional wailing women were paid to do the wailing. In this case, the bride merely cried and sighed. The groom also remained quiet and impassive throughout the process.

THE FAREWELL PARTY

In old Russia, this was not merely a party for the bride's friends, but a series of rituals. It was the time for the preparation of her "beauty", a small object that symbolized her life as a single woman.

The "beauty" could be a bit of wood decorated by ribbons and bits of cloth, a wreath, or a shawl. After the "beauty" was prepared, it was burned or given to the bride's closest friend. Whatever the object was, it was always connected symbolically with hair. Hair, traditionally, is a kind of personification of a maiden's beauty and self-will. By burning it, or giving it away, she symbolically lost her maidenhood.

Then she was washed in a steam room (a metaphor for death and rebirth), and this finished the farewell party. The bride would be led out of the steam room "neither alive nor dead," and in this state she was passed to the groom, though the bride and her friends continued to resist until the last.

BRUSHING THE BRIDE'S HAIR

Immediately after the wedding, the bride's hair was ritually brushed and plaited. Instead of a single braid, her hair was divided into two. The two braids were then tied into a bun on the back of her head, and a special head covering proper to a married woman (these varied by region) was put on her head.

From this moment, only the husband could see the hair of his wife. To appear with an uncovered head in front of another man was the same as adultery, while to tear the head covering off a woman's head was a terrible insult.

All this was symbolic of her change of status. At this point, the bride began to "come to life" again. She was given the right to move about freely and to do housework. When she entered her new home, she immediately began to feel out her new space.

THE AWAKENING OF THE BRIDE

A separate ritual was dedicated to the "awakening" of the bride when she arrived in her new home. It had two meanings. For the bride, it meant the return of her "sight." The bride, continuing to come back to life, now saw everything with new eyes. This was the first time that the bride and the groom both can see the beloved in the other, where before, there was no joy in the process.

Sometimes at this point a pie with no filling would be placed on her head. This symbolized her coming pregnancy. This pie was then wrapped up and placed in a closed-off room, where the young people at first ate the pie, then spent their first night together. In some regions, the bridal bed was set up in a barn, which was also associated with fertility.

THE FAREWELL

The young people then visited the bride's parents. This was a symbolic end to the wedding. The event was especially important for the bride, who came now as a guest to her former house, and not for long. It underlined the irrevocability of all the transformations that occurred during the wedding.

~

So much for the ritual aspect. What about the proper time for a wedding? In the consciousness of old Russian peasants, October 1, the feast of the Protection of the Mother of God, was a moment of passage between fall and winter.

"Before the Protection—autumn, after the Protection— here comes winter!" That's what they used to say in Russia. This day is also close to the first snowfall of the year—a time pregnant with significance and potential.

As strange as this may sound, village weddings were only performed *after* the celebration of the Protection (this assumes that the new year begins in September, according to the ecclesiastical calendar). The new reality of married life provoked different reactions from different people. Thinking of how the much-labored-over harvest was going to go to waste at the wedding banquet, the fathers of the bride would complain: "Old grandfather October! The only thing you're good for is reaching the bottom of a beer bottle."

Of course, young women had a quite different reaction. For them, the first of the month was a longed-for day, a celebration that they anticipated the whole year. On the morning of the first, young women came outside while it was still dark and began to sing:

 O Father-Protection, cover our Mother Earth and me as well. The white snow covered the earth; will it not also adorn me for marriage? O Father-Protection, cover the land with snow, but give me a husband!

In other places, the young women sang to "Mother-Protection."

Then the girls would go to church in the morning and light a candle before the icon of the Protection. In Belarus, they would add a special half-prayer, half-invocation: "Holy Protection! You who have covered the earth and the water, protect me as well!"

If the day brought snow, it was good luck for any who got married. If not, the bride could expect trouble: "If Protection (that is, the snow) didn't cover her head, the Nativity certainly won't!" they used to say in the villages.

Here's a typical incantation-prayer of a young woman before marriage:

> Leader-Mother-Mother of God, lead us to the other side (i.e. the foreign space of the husband's home); Greeter-Mother-Mother of God, meet me there on the other side.

This confusion of three major feasts of the Mother of God —The Protection, the Entrance into the Temple, and the Meeting in the Temple—is typical of such folk traditions.

In some areas, the young women would gather together on a day before the Protection, sing the proper songs, and weave a complete wedding veil over the course of the day. Before the morning liturgy, they would come to church and offer the veil before the icon of the Protection. Whispering, they would pray,

> Mother of God! Cover me quickly! Send me a husband with wit! O Protection of Christ, cover my poor head with a pearly cover (*kokoshnik*, a festal head covering), with a golden veil!

If a girl was lucky enough to get married on the Protection, the entire village would sing their dear girl to the church, sharing in that special joy.

Nowadays, there's still a strong connection between the feast of the Protection and wedding days. Many young, pious couples wait for this day to marry. Although they might not be able to tell you why, it's all connected to the old folk traditions surrounding the day's festivities.

CHAPTER 5
LOST CODES OF BEHAVIOR

I grew up in a conventional family. As social media seems to be highlighting an ever-increasing chaos all over the world, I've been thinking of how universal conventions of behavior have almost completely disappeared here in the US. And it occurred to me how much easier it would be for people if there were conventions of behavior we could all agree on. It would fix a lot of problems people have in relating to each other in romance, in conflict, in business, in life in general.

People in my fantasy novels don't act like freewheeling modern people. They live in regimented, rule-bound worlds. And do you know what? They like it.

Here is a list of some conventions from old Russia that might surprise you. Why can't you hold hands while dancing? What does it mean when you kiss someone on the shoulder? In front of what sort of a person should you bow to the ground? Or when should you just bow from the waist down?

Here are some of the answers:

THE HANDSHAKE

Shaking hands is so normal to us, we don't even think about it. But we forget that it's first of all a touch of skin on skin. It's a mutual "letting in" into an intimate space. In old Rus, people believed a touch could heal or curse. A touch could spark sexual attraction.

So, in 16th century Russia, you were not allowed to hold hands while doing line dances in the village. It was considered "a means to sensuality". The gesture of a handshake also had a second meaning in village life. It was a ritual "seal" on an agreement.

In North Russia, this ritual agreement took on cultic significance. A shepherd had to go into the woods every spring to make a deal with the *leshy*, the spirit of the forest. The deal was for the number of cows or sheep that would be dedicated to the *leshy*, which would guarantee an excellent pasture for the rest of the season. The shepherd had to shake the hand of the *leshy*. But touching evil spirits would inevitably lead to being cursed. So what to do?

He would put on thick woolen gloves, and he would add a special added glove made of straw to his right hand. This was "added protection" against the impurity of evil spirits. Even the handshake during the engagement between married couples had to be done with gloved hands, or someone might curse the wellbeing of the future couple. Shaking with ungloved hands was a sign of extreme trust, and so done very rarely.

THE KISS

Like the handshake, the kiss is a gesture with many possible meanings. A platonic, even ritualistic, kiss expresses a desire for health and wholeness. In Russian, the word for kiss has "tsel" as its root—the word for "whole." So the kiss is etymologically connected with the idea of prosperity and fullness. Not surprisingly, it was most proper to greet a guest with a kiss in old Russia.

By the 17th century, there was even a complicated kissing ritual that often flabbergasted foreign visitors. It involved a mutual exchange of bows, the drinking of a common cup of wine, and the wife of the host kissing all guests on the mouth. This ritual kiss was performed both when entering and when leaving the house.

The parting kiss was a seal of mutual forgiveness of offenses. The greeting kiss was similar to a kiss of honor, especially if you were visiting someone who had recently increased in social prestige. In Russia, those who were especially honored had their hands kissed, or even their feet!

A kiss on the shoulder was customary for a subordinate when greeting a superior. The superior's proper response was a kiss on the head. You can still see this when lower clergy takes a blessing from a priest or a bishop, especially in Russia.

Kissing the monarch's hand was an action given extreme importance. Only Christian ambassadors were allowed this honor. Non-Christians, Turks, and Tatars were explicitly prohibited from kissing the Tsar's hand. The official granting of the hand to kiss was proclaimed aloud to the ambassadors as a special grace of the Tsar, and an especially honored boyar would hold the hand while the ambassadors kissed it.

THE BOW

A bow of the head was exchanged as a simple greeting in Rus. It was also a fitting expression of gratitude. Among the peasants, it was customary to bow to the ground before a priest or a rich fellow peasant. This was called the "great rite". Bowing from the waist down (the "small rite") was a greeting for an equal. You would bow thus when entering another hut. A wife would greet her husband thus in the morning. Women bowed to men, and men to women (though men were allowed to not answer a woman's bow).

When you bowed your head, it had an important second meaning. You were, effectively, offering your life to the other person, to do with as they will. You were also willingly abasing yourself before your equal, offering him a higher status than yourself.

THE HEAD COVERING

Head coverings had some practical significance, but their symbolism was more important. The lack of a hat in a grown man was considered a sign of poverty. Social outcasts did not wear hats. This was because after marriage, men were not supposed to appear in public without a hat, just as a woman should never appear in public after marriage without a head covering. If a man ever had to take his hat off, it was only to show honor:

- when he meets a superior
- going to church
- kissing an icon, etc.

A woman, on the other hand, was never to take her head covering off, even in church. As you read in a previous chapter, a woman covered her head as a sign of hiding her beauty for all except her husband. In some places, the groom even had to "buy" her "beauty" (i.e. a false braid made of ribbons, representing her maidenhood). To forcibly take off the head covering of a woman who is not your wife was the worst kind of insult.

POSITION

In a society built on hierarchy, the status of every person depended on his relationship to those who were above and below him. In Russia, this social system was called *"mestnichestvo,"* literally "arrangement of places." This placement governed the rules of everything from table settings to service in the Tsar's court. The more honored the man, the closer his physical position would be to the Tsar or prince.

Arguing over "position" was also found in other social classes, even among the peasants. Or *especially* among the peasants. In fact, it was village life, with its ancient system of seating at official tables that gave rise to the social system of *mestnichestvo* among the nobles.

Connected with the proper standing or sitting position were the rules that governed who could sit in whose presence. Standing, socially speaking, was a sign of instability and ambiguity. A person of low social caste had to stand, while the privileged could sit. Thus, sitting, as a position of stability and lack of movement, was a sign of princely power. Sitting was connected with such ideals as happiness, fate, fortune. This is why:

- any good host always tries to get his guest to sit down before anything else
- no one should ever hurry to stand up from the dinner table
- all Russians (still) sit down in silence "for the road" before leaving on a journey.

CHAPTER 6
MYTHS ABOUT RUSSIAN CUISINE

A few years ago, I had the pleasure of taking part in amazing trip to Saratov, Russia, where I was one of 41 men recording sacred music for a men's choir CD. (That CD ended up being nominated for a Grammy). One of the more surprising aspects of the trip was the food. It was *actually* good. And this despite it being a fasting period.

This attitude toward Russian food, turns out, is widespread among Americans. A little while ago, some friends of mine got into a discussion about Russian cuisine. Most of the opinions were something like this—Russian food is terrible, boring, tasteless, fatty. But then someone made an important point. All the bad things people hear about Russian food are more properly referred to as Soviet problems.

He was right. Here are some of the most widespread myths about Russian cuisine:

THE POST-SOVIET MYTH: RUSSIAN FOOD IS FATTY AND UNINSPIRED

Seventy years of Soviet life have created this myth. Or rather, this is definitely true of Soviet cuisine, but not Russian cuisine in a wider historical sense. Soviet cuisine uses lots of mayonnaise, oils, fatty sausages, sardines, margarine—everything that would maximize a Soviet citizen's caloric intake from the minimum amount of food eaten.

But in 1913, which historians generally consider the year of Russia's peak of cultural development, the cuisine was completely different. There were many competing restaurants and eateries, with Moscow at the center of a bustling culinary culture. The highest aristocrats from Petersburg came to Moscow for special culinary tours, including stops at the famous public houses of Testov, Gurin, Egorov, and the Saratov Restaurant.

The variety of dishes in these places was staggering. Here's a typical menu from the restaurant of the merchant Guliarovskii: "piglet wrapped in dough, lobster soup with small pies, cream of wheat made with heavy cream (Gurievskaia), *botvinia* (a cold, fermented soup) with sturgeon, white cured fish fillet, *baidak* pie (a huge savory pie with a twelve-layer filling, everything from eel livers to beef brains) in a brown butter sauce.

THE PEASANT MYTH: RUSSIAN CUISINE IS TOO SIMPLISTIC

There's a Russian proverb: "Cabbage soup and porridge—that's all we need to eat". It's true that perhaps a peasant from Tambov could live mostly on turnips and porridge, but in many regions, before the Revolution, even peasants ate well. This was especially true of the areas around the capital and in Siberia. As proof, we have the writings of foreign travelers.

Take, for example, the travel journal of Marco Foscarino (1537):

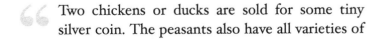 Two chickens or ducks are sold for some tiny silver coin. The peasants also have all varieties of

meat. In the winter, meat can survive for an entire month. They have wonderful fowl, which they catch with nets or with falcons (they have very good breeds here). Near the Volga, huge and delicious fish are served, especially sturgeon. The white lakes give a great variety of large and small fish of varying quality.

THE MYTH FROM NATURE: RUSSIAN CUISINE USES FEW FRUITS BECAUSE OF THE LONG WINTER

That's simply nonsense. Even Pierre Bezuhov (in *War and Peace*) cultivated pineapples in his hothouses. Practically anyone who was anyone had greenhouses or hothouses. The common people had a million ways of preserving berries and fruits for the entirety of winter in ways that preserved their nutrient content. These included baking, preserving in honey, freezing, or drying. Even the *Domostroi* (a document more famous for its questionable advice concerning husband-wife relations than its recipes) included recipes for preservation of fruits:

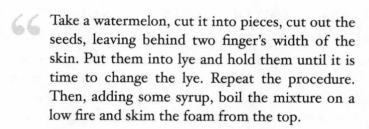

> Take a watermelon, cut it into pieces, cut out the seeds, leaving behind two finger's width of the skin. Put them into lye and hold them until it is time to change the lye. Repeat the procedure. Then, adding some syrup, boil the mixture on a low fire and skim the foam from the top.

THE MYTH OF FASTING: RUSSIAN CUISINE IS TASTELESS

This may be partially true of some fasting dishes, as many people who search old recipes find out. But the point of Lent is to eat simply. However, this is not characteristic of Russian cuisine in general. In many regions, dishes were seasoned extensively. Coastal cuisine, for example, added *volozhi* to all dishes. These were sauces in which food was cooked, baked, or garnished. There was a huge variety to these *volozhi*. Some were based on sour cream or butter, some were based on berries. Rich kitchens routinely used spiced lemon sauces.

THE MYTH FROM FOLKLORE: RUSSIAN CUISINE IS ARCHAIC

Yes, traditionally speaking, Russian cuisine had been rather one-note. This is because of the universal prevalence of the Russian oven, which led to the majority of dishes being baked (whether fish, fowl, or meat). However, in the city culture of the 19th century, this opposite was true.

There were many French chefs working in Russian restaurants, which did not mean that they imported French styles. Rather, they experimented with traditional Russian styles. Russian officers also brought back with them (after wars) various foods that now are considered typically Russian. This kind of "fusion" cuisine includes such delicacies as pastries, charlotte pies, veal Orloff, crepes with oysters, as well as the now world-famous salad created by Lucien Olivier in the famous Hermitage Restaurant.

CHAPTER 7
LOST IN TRANSLATION

One of the great challenges and joys for professional translators is to see how common words change their meaning over time. Sometimes, the meaning changes so much that you might think you were speaking a different language entirely.

Here are some of the strangest words and expressions in Russian that have become "lost in translation"

БУМАЖНИКЪ

Bumazhnik: "wallet"

This word is often found in old Russian sources. There, it means "cotton felt" or "padded mattress." This is probably because the word *"bumaga"* (paper) comes from the late Latin word *bombacium*, which means "cotton." The kind of paper you write on only appeared in Rus in the 15th century, quickly replacing birchbark and parchment. But "paper" in the sense of "official document" appeared in Russian even later.

ЖИРЪ

Zhir: "fat"

This word is actually connected to the word *"zhyt'"*, to live. It used to mean "riches, abundance, excess, luxury." Fat, as in fatty tissue, used to be called by a different word: *"tuk"*. *"Zhir,"* on the contrary, had a positive connotation. That's why many ancient Russian boys' names have "zhir" as the root: Zhiroslav, Zhirovit, Domazhir, Nazhir, Zhirochka.

In the "Lay of Igor's Campaign," Igor figuratively "drowns the fat of Russia" (*zhir*) in the Polovetsian river Kayala. In other words, he destroys the riches of the Russian lands in his ill-advised war.

Shades of this old meaning remain in sayings, such as *"Ne do zhiru, byt' by zhivu"* (i.e. "Not in luxury, but at least alive"). Of course, any positive association with the word *"zhir"* is long gone. Take, for example, Osip Mandelstam's use of the word *"zhir"* to call Stalin's fingers "fat, like worms."

ЗАДНИЦА

Zadnitsa: "buttocks"

The words *"peredny"* and *"zadny"* (front and back, respectively) had metaphorical meanings in old Russian, connected with time. Usually, *"peredny"* meant "the future," while *"zadny"* meant "the past." However, the opposite was also sometimes true. For example, the word *"zadnitsa"* meant "that which is left behind a man in his future." In other words, his inheritance.

This is a characteristically Slavic social term that appears often in the "Russian Law," the official code of laws of Kievan Rus. There is even a special section "On the *Zadnitsa*". Here's a quote:

If brothers quarrel before the prince concerning their inheritance (*zadnitsa*)..."

Land that was left without anyone to inherit was called *"bezzadnitsa"* (in modern Russia, this sounds like "someone without a butt"). Some historians sheepishly change the accent in the word to the second-to-last syllable, even though it's clear from the original manuscripts that the word sounded exactly the same as it does now.

ЗДОРОВЫЙ

Zdorovy: "healthy"

In old Rus, this word meant "successful," because it's etymologically connected with a word that means "built from a good piece of wood." Because of this, we find the astounding quote (to modern ears) in the fourth chronicle of Novgorod:

> И приидоша вси здорови, но ранени, а Иван Клекачевич превезен преставися с тои раны.
> And so came all the wounded from among the triumphant. Ivan Klekachevich, upon being brought, died of his wounds.

The astounding part is the first phrase "wounded from among the triumphant." If translated using modern Russian, it would have sounded "And so came all the healthy, but wounded."

ПРИНИМАТЬ (ПРИИМАТИ)

Prinimat': "to accept"

The old Russian version of this word had many meanings. As with *"peredny"* and *"zadny,"* some of these meanings actually contradicted each other. For example, it could mean "to host a guest," but it could also mean "to arrest." Interestingly, this old usage can actually be heard in some modern slang: "they've hosted (i.e. locked up) the guys" (ребят приняли) appears in some gangster films.

In the Russian translation of Josephus's history of the Jewish Wars, we find an interesting phrase. A certain person "accepted the best people," but also "accepted the worst." This phrase doesn't exist in the original Greek. If this is a corruption of the text, it shows how easily Russians used the same word in opposite meanings. This may also have something to do with Russians' uncommon ability to pun (but that's a different story altogether).

УБИТЬ (УБИТИ)

Ubit': "to kill"

This word used to mean not just "to kill until dead," but "to beat badly." One of the most horrifying surviving artifacts from old Rus (written on birch) is the letter of a battered woman. She writes "with tears" to a powerful relative:

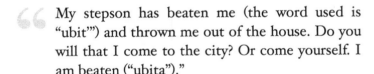

> My stepson has beaten me (the word used is "ubit'") and thrown me out of the house. Do you will that I come to the city? Or come yourself. I am beaten ("ubita")."

ХОТЕТЬ (ХОТЕТИ)

Khotet': "to want, to desire"

This word used to be a helping verb in old Russian. It indicated future tense or an action that cannot be undone. You could "*khotet'*" the most unusual of things. In the "Chronicle of Past Times," the people in a besieged city seem to be saying that they want to die from hunger, and the prince won't help them. Of course, they don't want to die. What they're actually saying is that their death is an inevitability if the prince does not come and help them.

CHAPTER 8
BIZARRE RUSSIAN PHRASES

I t would have been bad enough to have untranslatable words. But any good student of languages knows the peculiar wonder of popular expressions or folk sayings. Personally, I've always appreciated the cultural richness that is hinted at by these expressions. They not only tell a story, but they reveal a lost world that only a few remember or even know about. Here are some of the most interesting Russian phrases you will still hear spoken sometimes.

ИВАН РОДСТВА НЕ ПОМНЯЩИЙ—IVAN WHO DOESN'T REMEMBER HIS FAMILY

It means someone who doesn't like to follow traditions or rules. An innovator (not in a good way). The historical meaning is this. During Tsarist times, the police had to deal with runaway prisoners, serfs who were trying to escape hard masters, soldiers who couldn't finish boot camp, various sectarians, and other wanderers with no official papers. These people often hid their real names and places of residence. If asked about their names, they all called themselves "Ivan," and claimed they didn't remember their families.

ТОЛОЧЬ ВОДУ В СТУПЕ—TO BEAT WATER IN A MORTAR

It means "to beat the air," to waste time doing something useless. The hidden meaning has to do with the supposedly miraculous properties of water. From pagan times, Russians were in awe of water. People used to whisper blessings on water and wait for miracles. But what if someone had already mumbled something over the water? Especially if that someone swore when he dropped a jug of it? Water remembers everything!

So the old pagan priests found a way to "erase" the negative information from water. They used to beat water in a vessel for a long time. After a few days of torturing the water, the water was ready to be whispered over and used for magical rites. The druids would use the supposedly magic water for barter. But eventually, people realized that the water didn't do anything special. So after a long time, this became an expression meaning "to waste your time."

ШУТ ГОРОХОВЫЙ—A PEA-GREEN JESTER

It's a derogatory expression: "stupid idiot," or "moron." The image of the jester of Medieval Europe is well known—wearing motley, a hat with donkey ears, holding a rattle in his hand (the rattle was often a bull bladder filled with dried peas). He would always begin his performances by rattling the peas. In Russia, jesters liked to decorate themselves with dried stalks of pea plants. During the folk celebrations before Lent, an effigy of a pea-green jester was carried around on the streets.

ТЯНУТЬ КАНИТЕЛЬ—TO SPIN GOLD THREAD

It means to do humdrum work. To work a long time at a monotonous task. So why do you need to spin gold thread?

Metal threads, whether of silver or gold, were used in decorations of clothing and rugs. To make it "sewable," you had to make it extremely thin by beating it and pulling it through smaller and smaller holes. The process was laborious and very, very boring.

ДЕЛИТЬ ШКУРУ НЕУБИТОГО МЕДВЕДЯ—TO DIVIDE THE PELT OF A LIVING BEAR

An English equivalent might be "to count your chickens before they hatch." The older version of this phrase is "to sell the pelt of a living bear." The meaning is pretty clear—you shouldn't make plans before you've planned properly. The source of the bear image is actually from a French fable called "The Bear and Two Companions" by Jean de La Fontaine. The story concerns two fur traders who make a bargain for the pelt of a bear they haven't killed yet. Hilarity ensues. You can read the full fable online.

СЪЕСТЬ СОБАКУ—TO EAT A DOG

The phrase now means to go through bitter experience, and come out the wiser. But originally, the phrase was ironic. Here's the full version: "He ate the dog, but choked on the tail." The expression was used to laugh at someone who had finished a very difficult job, but tripped up at the end over some trifle.

ВЫНОСИТЬ СОР ИЗ ИЗБЫ—TO CARRY THE GARBAGE OUT OF THE HUT

Translation: "to air out your dirty laundry". This one also goes back to pagan rites. The thing is, garbage was never carried to a public garbage dump. It was usually burned in the stove. Why? People believed that a magician could find out a family's secrets by smelling their garbage. If he really wanted to harm them, he could even bury the garbage in a cemetery (not good!)

ДЕЛУ ВРЕМЯ И ПОТЕХЕ ЧАС—THERE'S A TIME FOR WORK, AND A TIME FOR PLAY

This one might seem obvious, but there's an interesting historical episode here. In 17th century Russia, the most popular way for a noble to spend his free time was hunting with falcons. Even Tsar Alexei Mikhailovich loved it—he hunted almost every day, except for winter. He even published a set of rules for proper falconry.

In this rulebook, the hunt was praised as an occupation that was very good at banishing sorrow and misfortunes. However, ultimately the Tsar decided that people had started enjoying it too much, and government business was suffering. So at the end of his rulebook, he added a warning: "Do not forget the business of government: there is a time for work, and a time for play."

КУДА МАКАР ТЕЛЯТ НЕ ГОНЯЕТ—WHERE EVEN MAKAR WON'T TAKE HIS COWS

Translation: very, very far away. Here's one version of this saying's provenance. Peter the Great was traveling through Riazan'. He liked to talk to the common people incognito. It so happened that on a certain day, every peasant he met just happened to be named "Makar". The Tsar was surprised by this, then was reputed to say, "From this day forth, you shall all be called Makar!" From that time, the name "Makar" was used as a catchphrase for "peasant man."

ТАНЦЕВАТЬ ОТ ПЕЧКИ—TO DANCE FROM THE STOVE

Strangely enough, this expression means "to act always in the same way, never changing based on newly-acquired knowledge." Funny story: a certain man named Sergei Terebenev returned to Russia after a long absence abroad. When he returned, full of nostalgia, he recalled his childhood memories of taking dance classes.

So he's standing at the stove, his feet in "position three." His parents and servants are standing around watching him. The teacher gives the command: "One, two, three." Sergei does the first step, but loses his beat, and his feet get tangled up.

His father says, "O, what a mess! Well, get back to the stove, start dancing again!"

ЗАРУБИТЬ НА НОСУ—TO HACK AT THE NOSE

This one sounds more violent than it actually is. It means to remember something forever. The image that comes to mind is a poor schoolboy that's standing in front of an angry teacher who threatens him with a finger again and again. The poor boy imagines it's an axe hacking away at his nose. But that's not it at all. Actually, a "nose" is a small wooden board notched by illiterate peasants as a way of remembering important tasks.

СЕМЬ ПЯТНИЦ НА НЕДЕЛЕ—SEVEN FRIDAYS A WEEK

This describes a person who constantly changes his mind. Someone you can't trust. In old times, Friday was market day. Everyone shopped on a Friday. Friday was the day that the goods arrived, and payment was arranged for the followed market day (Friday). Whoever did not come through with the payment was branded with this expression: "For that guy, it's seven Fridays a week!"

But there's a different explanation too. Workers were usually allowed to leave early on a Friday, so a lazy bum was also given this expression. For him, every day was a day off, so to speak.

ВИЛАМИ НА ВОДЕ НАПИСАНО—WRITTEN ON WATER WITH A PITCHFORK

Translation: "a very doubtful event." There are two explanations for this expression. "Vila" (the Russian word for pitchfork) is also another name for mermaids, dangerous spirits who were said to drown young men. If you saw them writing on the water, you could be sure that what they wrote would come true.

The second meaning refers to pitchforks as ritual objects used by pagan priests. The three points of the fork were said to symbolize the essence of the god Triglav (literally, three-headed one). Druids would use them to "draw" runes on water as part of their magic rites. Of course, when nothing happened, people started to give the action its opposite meaning.

ОТРЕЗАННЫЙ ЛОМОТЬ—A CUT-OFF PIECE OF BREAD

This refers to someone who has become independent—a daughter given to a husband who lives very far away, or a son whose started his own family and never comes to visit his parents.

Interestingly, in old times bread was never cut, because it symbolized life. You were only supposed to break pieces off. So the expression "cut-off piece of bread" is a real historical oxymoron.

CHAPTER 9
THE RUSSIAN ROSETTA STONE

Have you read Evgenii Vodolazkin's excellent novel *Laurus*? If you haven't, you've deprived yourselves of a rare experience of serious, contemplative fiction in the grand tradition of Christian humanism. (See my review if you need an extra push). Those of you who read it will probably remember the main character's most prized possession. It's the thing that grounds him, that gives him meaning in a world of plague and chaos. Ultimately, it's also the thing he must abandon on his path toward sanctity.

What is it? It's a bag full of notes written on birch bark. Everything from excerpts from a popular novel about Alexander the Great to the writings of the Holy Fathers to practical advice about treating common ailments—it's all there. It turns out that these birch notes aren't some fiction invented by the author. They are a historical reality. More than that, they are a kind of Rosetta Stone for Medieval Rus.

I use the term Rosetta Stone loosely here, to mean a key to a cypher. In 1951, an archaeological expedition in Novgorod found a treasure trove of these birch notes, and they became a historical sensation. They completely changed the historical thinking surrounding the everyday life of medieval Russians.

NOTES ON EVERYDAY LIFE

Until this expedition, most historical knowledge concerning medieval Russians came from reading the Chronicles or juridical texts. Clearly, these aren't very good at describing daily life, because they dealt with "great men"—princes, nobility, clergy. But what about common people living their daily lives in the middle ages? What about the city dwellers, the peasants, the merchants, the artisans? All information about them had to be extrapolated from juridical texts; however, those deal not with concrete individuals, but social functions.

The birch notes opened a window into the actual everyday lives of the "not so great" men and women. First of all, these are extremely practical items. When a medieval Russian took up a stylus to write on a bit of birch bark, he did it because of practical necessity. For example, a merchant is traveling, and he decides to write a letter to his family. Or an artisan decides to write a formal complaint against a customer.

An interesting conundrum arises for the historian, however. As a rule, people used personal names in these notes. We find nothing about their social status. For example, someone named Miliata writes to his brother. At first, it's unclear who he is. Only contextually can a historian figure out that he's a merchant. Or when someone named Miroslav writes to Olisei Grechin, it's not immediately apparent that the first is a nobleman and the second a lawyer. But these difficulties aside, now the life of medieval Rus comes to life in vivid color and great detail.

Interestingly, in Scandinavian countries of the same time period, people wrote on wooden boards, not birch. In Rus, it was mostly a matter of tradition. Literacy spread widely after the acceptance of Christian faith and culture. The Christian tradition was preserved and disseminated in books of parchment, and in some sense, birch bark looks and feels like parchment. As for the Scandinavians, their Runic system of writing came before their acceptance of Christianity, and for many centuries they had already had a tradition of etching out runes on wooden boards.

THE SCHOOL OF YAROSLAV THE WISE

The earliest birch notes date to the beginning of the 11th century, not long after Rus was baptized. So how did so many people become literate in such a relatively short period of time? It turns out that the generation that was young when Rus was baptized were specially prepared to be a literate generation of Christians for a "new Rus." Prince Yaroslav of Novgorod opened a school in 1030. As the *Chronicles* have it:

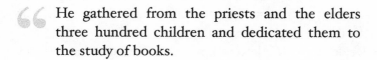 He gathered from the priests and the elders three hundred children and dedicated them to the study of books.

Interestingly, this school made it into Scandinavian epic poetry. In the Saga of Olaf Tryggvason, the main character actually visits the school when he comes to see Yaroslav. So these three hundred children learned to read and write and became the educated elite of Novgorodian society. They formed a social foundation for the spread of literacy. They taught their own friends and, eventually, their children, and soon literacy was widespread.

GARBAGE DUMPS?

More than that, merchants immediately recognized the usefulness of literacy. Before Rus's baptism, they drew accounts by drawing pictures, not using words. These birch notes became so universal, that people just started throwing them out like garbage after they were finished.

The paradox is that this is exactly why the notes were

preserved to this day. Books that were carefully protected often were destroyed in fires (which happened fairly regularly). But those items that people just threw out were trampled into the dirt, and in Novgorod, the soil preserves organic material very well.

This interesting fact allowed historians to find the places where Novgorodians set up their garbage dumps. It was wherever they found a large concentration of birch bark notes.

Sometimes these birch notes were mailed great distances. For example, five letters have been found, belonging to a certain merchant named Luke to his father. In one, he writes that he is traveling from the North, and he complains that in the North, they sold squirrel furs at exorbitant prices, so he didn't buy any. In another letter, he wrote from the region of the Dniepr River where he was sitting and waiting for a *grechnik*. That word technically refers to buckwheat, but in the local slang, it meant a Greek caravan from Byzantium (Grek is "Greek" in Russian).

Here's yet another example. A son writes to his mother, "Come here, either to Smolensk or Kiev, because bread is cheap here."

THE BOY ONPHIM

A famous example of birch notes from that time is a boy's drawing where he depicts himself as St. George killing the dragon. Some say that this note is an actual page from a school notebook, meaning that even in the 11-12th century, there were already textbooks used in schools. In fact, it's clear that sometimes birch notes were sewn together to make notebooks, even early on.

For example, there's an example of a small booklet of sewn-together birch notes that contain the evening prayers. On the flip side, books of magic from the Greeks or the Copts were very popular at that time, and you find many of them still preserved. The most popular is called the "Legend of Sisinius," which is basically a book of spells to protect a mother and her newborn child from evil spirits.

This boy, named Onphim, actually had many notes preserved. There's a particularly funny one where he begins to write the text of a prayer, but in the middle of a word, he suddenly begins to write down the alphabet. It comes out something like this: "For He is greatly-b-c-d-e."

THE FATE OF THE MONASTERY'S COW

Interestingly, our knowledge of daily church life also increased because of these birch bark notes. At first, most of the recovered notes seemed only secular in nature. But about twenty years after the first ones were found, a new series of notes were uncovered. They included lists of church feasts for the autumn and even the order of the Paschal service. It turns out these were scribblings written down by parish priests for their daily needs.

Another interesting one dating to the 13th century is a long list of sins. Either it was a preparation for confession, or a "cheat sheet" for the priest's Sunday sermon. None of these notes are scholarly in nature. No abstract theology is present here. Instead, we find all the practical daily necessities of a priest's life.

There's one fascinating example where we find the same handwriting in a fragment of a church calendar and a letter written from Liudslav to Khoten. It's likely that Liudslav was illiterate and came to the priest to ask him to transcribe a personal letter for him. This also shows that the clergy in Novgorod were not isolated from the rest of the populace. They lived side-by-side with their charges and their way of thinking influenced the writing style even in secular notes.

For example, many letters from that time begin with the word "I bow to you," and end with "I greet you with a kiss."

The similarities to St. Paul's epistles are clear (Romans 16:16), and this tradition clearly originated in the ecclesiastical sphere.

One of the more interesting collection of notes comes from the place where a woman's monastery stood in the 12th century. It was built right in the middle of the city, in no way separated from the houses and yards of the surrounding merchants and boyars. Some of the notes found here were clearly written by nuns:

> As for the three bits of cloth for the head covering, please send them over quickly."
>
> "Can you find out if Matthew is in the monastery?" (in context, it seems Matthew is the priest)
>
> "Is St. Barbara's heifer healthy?"

In this part of the city, mentions of God in everyday speech are also widespread. Instead of saying "Of course," people would say, "For God's sake." A common warning was "fear God." It's entirely possible that the locals started speaking like this because they were so close to the monastery.

We also find an interesting fact about the clergy of the time. They didn't see themselves as a separate social class at all. For example, we already mentioned a certain Olisei Grechin. He was a fascinating character. On the one hand, he was a priest, but he was also an artist and an iconographer. But that didn't stop him from also being a central figure in the city's government. And his father was a boyar, not a priest.

Here's another interesting example from the early 15th century. It's a letter to Archbishop Simeon asking for a local deacon, Alexander, to be made priest:

> All the inhabitants of the Rzhevsk uezd in the region of Oshevsk, from the least to the greatest,

bow their heads to Vladyka Simeon. We beg that Deacon Alexander be made priest, for his father and his grandfather sang before the holy Mother of God in Oshev.

In other words, this was a local example of a "clergy dynasty."

THE DEEPLY PERSONAL

The influence of Christianity was everywhere felt. When people said "For God's sake" or "fear God," these were not simply figures of speech. At the same time, the old pagan mindset persisted for a long time. For example, one of the notes has this threat: "If you don't do what I asked you about, I will consign you to the Mother of God, to whom you swore an oath." In other words, on the one hand this person is appealing to ecclesiastical authority, but on the other hand, he uses the language of cursing, typical of a pagan.

Another example is a letter from the 11th century written by a young woman to the man she loved. She rebuked him in a way that sounds completely understandable to modern ears: "Did I offend you when I asked you to come to me?" The rest of the letter goes like this:

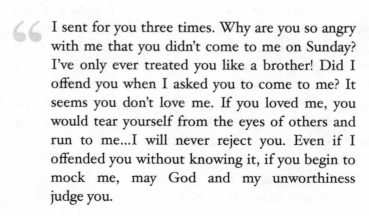

> I sent for you three times. Why are you so angry with me that you didn't come to me on Sunday? I've only ever treated you like a brother! Did I offend you when I asked you to come to me? It seems you don't love me. If you loved me, you would tear yourself from the eyes of others and run to me...I will never reject you. Even if I offended you without knowing it, if you begin to mock me, may God and my unworthiness judge you.

That expression "my unworthiness" is a literary expression that comes from a well-known Greek source. (Women were as well-educated as men at that time, in other words).

Sadly, this letter was torn by the recipient, tied together into a knot and thrown off a bridge.

The persistence of a pagan mindset was also seen in widespread spells that were half-incantations, half prayers, spoken against all manner of evils. Here's one that was supposed to guard against the flu:

> Thrice-nine (an expression reminiscent more of folk tales than of prayers -NK) angels, thrice-nine archangels, deliver the servant of God Micah from the shakes by the prayers of the Holy Theotokos.

All this is extremely interesting in our time, when the middle ages, a time of profound faith, are still routinely ridiculed as a "Dark Age." In actual fact, the coming of Christianity meant the coming of literacy and culture. It's something to think about as more and more people lambaste Christianity as a source of darkness and ignorance, when it has always been a source of education, illumination, and wisdom.

CHAPTER 10

INTERESTING FACTS ABOUT KIEVAN RUS

Th   hese days, Tolkien isn't particularly popular among
certain readers and publishers of fantasy. To be
called "Tolkien-esque" can even be slightly insulting,
as strange as that may sound. Still, Tolkien casts a wide shadow
on the genre, not least since he grounded his imaginative
world in real history. Nowadays, every good fantasy takes some
actual historical culture as its basis, whether it's China for Guy
Gavriel Kay or ancient Egypt for N. K. Jemisin.

Early Medieval Russia, the time period called "Kievan
Rus," is the historical setting for my fantasy world. It is a time
period shrouded in myth, making it a perfect setting for epic
fantasy. Still, there is enough real history to ground that
fantasy in gritty reality. I especially like to read about random
historical bits that have gotten lost in the cracks. A lot of them
are little stories in themselves. Here are some unexpected facts
about that semi-mythical time.

UNEXPECTED FACTS ABOUT "KIEVAN RUS"

It turns out that "Kievan Rus" as such never existed. The name
was a 19th century invention that corresponded to the nation-

alistic ideals of the Russian Empire. It was intended to evoke an ancient past where different cities were all unified under a single "Grand Prince." Actually, the principalities were independent, divided, and constantly at war. Even though the title "Grand Prince" was coveted, it was little more than an honorific.

ORTHODOX CHURCHES WITH...ORGANS?

It turns out that Russia, the land known for the peal of bells, initially may have had organs, not bells in its churches. Only large churches in major cities had bells. Although it should be noted that the evidence for this is scanty. One of the only suggestions of this is a fresco in the ancient Cathedral of St. Sophia in Kiev that shows jesters playing on organs in church. (Admittedly, not the most reliable of proofs!)

WHAT DID EARLY RUSSIAN PRINCES LOOK LIKE?

There's a definite "image" that Russian princes command in the imagination—tall, golden-haired, blue-eyed. Actually, that was probably not the case at all. Kiev and other principalities practiced political marriages from the very beginning. Not only Western European brides were chosen, but also brides from the various nomadic Asian tribes who constantly harassed the Russian cities. So sometimes Russian princes looked distinctly un-European.

THE VECHE: A DEMOCRATIC ASSEMBLY?

The Russian popular imagination has canonized the Veche, a democratic assembly of townspeople that elected rulers in some cities, especially Novgorod. In actual fact, there was little "democracy" about it. Most people in cities were not freemen, and had no civic rights whatsoever. Most of the time, the democratic "Veche" was little more than a council of nobles.

SLAVERY?

Yes, it's a little known fact, but one of the major sources of profit in old Rus was slavery. Selling foreign prisoners of war into slavery was a common practice, but some princes even sold other Slavs into slavery. Slavic prisoners were especially coveted in Eastern slave markets. Arabic manuscripts of the tenth and eleventh centuries describe in vivid detail how Slavic slaves traveled from Rus into the Caliphate and the Mediterranean. It often happened that if you owed money to someone higher up on the food chain, he could legally sell you to slave traders. It may seem strange that a Christian nation sold slaves, but actually most cities in Rus remained pagan until at least the 12th century.

KIEV—THE THIRD ROME

Before the Mongol invasions, Kiev was a wonder of the ancient world. It was larger than one square mile in size (massive for its time and place). There were hundreds of churches. It was the first city in Rus to have organized streets and quarters. It impressed European and Arabic visitors alike. Some Byzantines even compared it (obviously hyperbolizing) to Constantinople itself. But hardly anything remains from that glorious time, everything having been destroyed by the Mongols and later wars. Only the church of St. Sophia and a few reconstructed gates remain.

THE CYRILLIC ALPHABET WAS NEVER REALLY USED

Well, that's not quite true. The written language created by Cyrill and Methodius, which was the original "Cyrillic" alphabet (now called Glagolytic) never really took off. This alphabet was used as a code language, however, even after people had stopped using it as a written language. The first historical appearance of what is today called Cyrillic was a cryptic word (*"gorushna"*) on a clay urn. No one knows what that word means, even today.

ALCOHOLISM IS NOT A HISTORICALLY RUSSIAN TRAIT

Drinking strong alcohol was not something that early Russians did at all. Even wine only appeared in general use after the Mongol invasions (13th century and on). In fact, Kiev didn't even have breweries! Whatever "alcoholic" drinks were enjoyed—mead and kvass—rarely were stronger than 1% or 2% in alcohol content.

As for food, common people never ate some things we can't live without—butter, sugar, even mustard. Even tea (a staple in Russian homes) wasn't drunk. Instead, people boiled rosebay, something that's still done in some places, a drink now called Ivan Chai. They ate a lot of meat—pigeon, rabbit, venison, and wild boar. Also, they ate plenty of cheese and sour cream.

RUS WAS BAPTIZED IN... THE TWELFTH CENTURY?

Well, Prince Vladimir did baptize Kiev and the surrounding areas in 988-9. However, it was largely a local event. Polotsk was only baptized in the 11th century. As for Rostov and

Murom—they had a large population of pagan Finns—they were only baptized in the early 12th. A convincing proof of the slowness of Russian Christianization were the repeated revolts of pagan priests that were supported by large chunks of the population (one in Suzdal in 1024, one in Novgorod in 1071).

CHAPTER 11

NAMING CONVENTIONS

Any parent knows that naming a children is no small
task, not only because choosing names that both
parents will like is difficult enough, but because there
are all kinds of expectations heaped on children, and their
names are part of that. Turns out that this is not a new
problem.

The rules for naming a Russian prince in the early days of
Rus were even more complicated that the expectations
surrounding naming in our own time. If you want to give your
next child a name according to the proper rules of ancient Rus,
here they are!

DON'T GIVE YOUR SON THE NAME OF YOUR
FATHER OR GRANDFATHER, IF EITHER IS ALIVE

Repeating a name was considered dangerous, because the life
force of the living ancestor would leave and pass on to the
offspring who shared his name. So you should choose the name
of an appropriately dead ancestor. There is, however, one
exception. It is permissible—in some cases even desirable—to
name your child after a living uncle. This is a wonderful oppor-

51

tunity to lay the foundation for a good relationship between the child and his uncle. After all, according to old Russian traditions, it is the uncle who will take care of your child if you die.

YOU SHOULD NEVER GIVE YOUR SON YOUR OWN NAME

If you are Vladimir (or Volodimir, in proper old Rus fashion), you must not name your son Vladimir also. There were no Vladimir Vladimirovichi in Russia before the Mongols. If there ever was such a combination, it meant that the child was born after the father died. However, you can use part of your name. In the case of Volodimir, either "volod" or "mir" are appropriate, so you can call him Vsevolod or Miroslav (though the name Miroslav never appears in the lists of Russian princes, but still).

YOU CAN USE EXOTIC NAMES, SUCH AS SCANDINAVIAN NAMES THAT ARE NOT IN THE LIST OF RUSSIAN NAMES

Some Scandinavian saints were honored in Russia (St. Olaf of Norway, for example). There are suggestions that there was an old church in St. Olaf's honor built in Novgorod. In an ancient transcript of a prayer to the Holy Trinity (12th century), St. Olaf is mentioned together with St. Canute and St. Magnus of Orkney. So there you go. Name your son Canute. He's an Orthodox saint.

STILL, YOU SHOULD BE CAREFUL WITH FOREIGN NAMES

In old Rus, foreign names that were uncommon in one's family tree were often given to bastards. That doesn't mean that a Russian prince with a Scandinavian name couldn't inherit the throne, but there's always a chance that some people might grow suspicious and even oppose him. There's actually a historical example of this from 11th century Scandinavia. Olaf of Sweden, the father of Ingigerd (who became the wife of Yaroslav the Wise), called his lawful son Jacob, since he was born on the day of Apostle James.

This was not a Scandinavian name, but Olaf had only recently been baptized. As a zealous neophyte, he was eager to follow all the ancient rules of Christian naming. When Jacob, the son of Olaf, was supposed to become king of Sweden, his own people told him that his name was not kingly enough. Eventually, he was chosen as king, but given another dynastic name—Anund. Eventually, he was known by a double name (Anund Jacob), something very unusual for the Sweden of that time.

DON'T FORGET THAT NAMES HAVE MEANING

In the world of the Middle Ages, names carried great significance. Every name has its own subtext and its own cultural associations. For example, the name Izjaslav was often given to second sons of princely dynasties. However, it was not that unusual for first sons to die of natural causes, so the second son was not an insignificant figure in a princely family, almost an heir.

LOOK IN THE CHURCH CALENDAR

Princes in early Rus had two names—a dynastic name (pagan in origin) and a Christian name given at baptism. Each name had its proper place. In the church, no prince could say "the servant of God Izjaslav approaches communion," because there is no saint named Izjaslav. Christian names have their own rules and can be chosen in several ways.

You can choose to give your future prince the name of the saint commemorated on his day of birth or on the eighth day after birth (this is connected to the prayers of the eighth day, which in turn are based on the circumcision ritual of the Old Testament). Alternately, you can also choose the saint of the fortieth day after birth. However, you should keep in mind that the church calendar would only be checked after all other genealogical rules, rites, and habits were consulted first.

DON'T GIVE YOUR SON THE NAME OF A MARTYR OR OTHER PERSON WITH A DIFFICULT FATE

In Rus, an old belief persisted that a name is a sign that predetermines the fate of a child. Even as late as the 19th century, ethnographers noticed that Russian peasants really didn't like to give their children martyrs' names. Some even tried to bribe priests to baptize their children in honor of saints who died natural deaths. Although that is perhaps an extreme position, if you are intent on following these rules, you should not fail to study the lives of the saints whose names you like. Try to choose a patron with a fortunate end.

CHAPTER 12
HOW RUSSIAN PRINCES LIVED

I f the naming conventions surrounding the birth of a
prince weren't intense enough, the life he could expect to
live was perhaps even more bound by tradition and
convention.

BIRTH

We're all heard the stories of mothers giving birth in cabs on
the way to the hospital. Well, old Rus was no exception.
Except the cabs were caravans, and the trips took weeks, not
minutes or hours. So, in 1174, we have written evidence that
when Rurik Rostislavich traveled from Novgorod to Smolensk,
his wife gave birth.

Rurik then gave the village where his son was born to his
son as a birth-gift. He immediately commissioned that a
church be built on the spot, in honor of the Archangel
Michael. The founding of churches in honor of the heir's birth
was the prerogative of grand princes. Thus, for example,
Mstislav the Great built the church of the Annunciation in
Gorodishche. You can still see the ruins of that ancient church
today, near Novgorod. The choice of the Annunciation was

obvious—his son (Vsevolod) was given the baptismal name Gabriel, after the archangel who brought the good news to the virgin Mary.

Gabriel-Vsevolod, in his turn, built a church "in his son's name" dedicated to St. John the Baptist.

THE FIRST HAIRCUT

Tonsure (the ritual haircut) was a social practice found all over old Russia and other Slavic nations. We know from the chronicles that this ritual was performed at age two or three. Not only was this the first haircut, but it was also the first time the young prince was placed on a horse. Some historians also believe that the prince was also dressed in his first armor on this day.

Being put on a horse was symbolic. Now, the prince entered the adult life of the warrior. He symbolically demonstrated his physical ability, even at such a young age. It's interesting that in the same chronicles, old age is symbolically described in similar terms. A man is old when he can no longer sit astride a horse.

In the Novgorod Chronicle, we read that in 1230, Archbishop Spiridon of Novgorod himself cut the hair of Rostislav Mihailovich, son of the prince of Chernigov. This rite was performed in the cathedral of the Holy Wisdom, the most important church of the city.

THE "FIRST RULE"

The young prince began to practice at ruling very early. The already mentioned Rostislav Mihailovich, who had just been shorn, remained in Novgorod under the watch of the archbishop. When his father returned to Chernigov, Rostislav's presence in Novgorod was a sign of Chernigov's power over

Novgorod, and though the little boy did not rule, it was a de facto beginning of political life for him.

There is a moving account of Prince Vsevolod "Big Nest" (called this because he had LOTS of kids) sending his 17-year old to rule in Novgorod. The entire family, together with most of the city, accompanied him out of his home city. Prince Vsevolod gave him a cross ("the protector and helper") and a sword ("a threat to frighten"), along with his parting words as father and Grand Prince.

THE SON OF THE PRINCE AS HOSTAGE

It was not always pleasant to be the son of a prince. Sometimes, his childhood had to be spent in the military camp of a former enemy. This tradition was widespread in Western Europe as well, and is a constant plot point in Medieval fantasy literature.

The son of Vladimir Monomakh, Sviatoslav, was a hostage of the Polovetsian (an Asiatic nomad tribe) prince named Kitan. When Vladimir prepared to attack the Polovetsians, the most dangerous and urgent task was rescuing Sviatoslav first, because at the first sign of an attack, he would have been killed.

There were tragic stories as well. When Vsevolod "Big Nest" took Gleb, the son of Sviatoslav Vsevolodovich, as a hostage, Sviatoslav literally went mad. He began to attack many of his former allies to grab as many hostages for himself as he could. Luckily, the whole affair ended in the best possible way—a dynastic marriage.

HELPING HIS FATHER RULE

Princes were not always shipped off at a young age. Some spent their youth next to their fathers, actively taking part in his rule and military campaigns, learning by example. Usually, this was the preferred method of raising sons in a time of war.

THE WEDDING AND CHILDREN

A noble wedding (different from the peasant weddings already mentioned in a previous chapter) was always hosted by an elderly relative—the father, uncle, or even grandfather. Old Russian weddings had this unique feature: they often happened in pairs. Two brothers, two sisters, or two other close relatives celebrated at the same time.

People got married at an age we would consider early. For example, the daughter of Vsevolod "Big Nest", Verhuslava, married Rostislav, the son of Rurik Rostislavich when she was eight years old! But this was an exception, even for that time. The chronicle mentions that her father and mother were crying at the wedding. Rostislav was seventeen.

If everything went well, after the wedding, the groom's father-in-law would be as much his benefactor as his own father. Rostislav, for example, was a favorite of his father-in-law Vsevolod "Big Nest", who would give him various trophies of war and come to visit him for days on end. Sometimes, the father-in-law was even closer than a father.

Children, of course, were a big deal. Not only did they continue the line, but they were political capital, in some sense. For example, Prince Viacheslav Vladimirovich was considered vulnerable by his enemies because he had no grown sons. For this reason, he was excluded from active political life. Some of the boyars even said of him, "He will not be able to hold Kiev."

However, having too many sons was also a problem, especially since all sons had to receive land and power. It led to the period known as the Internecine Wars, when brothers killed brothers for a better city.

THE DEATH OF THE FATHER

This was a major milestone. Here are some of the important issues surrounding such a death:

- Did your father manage to spend at least some time on the Grand Princely throne of Kiev?
- Did he leave you a good reputation among his subjects?
- How do his brothers look at you?
- Who are your sisters married to?

Here's an example: Iziaslav Mstislavich was not in the greatest position to inherit the Grand Princely throne because he was not first in line. However, his sisters and nieces were married to major players in Europe and Russia. This played a role in his eventually successful ploy to rule Kiev, Mother of Russian Cities.

Immediately after a prince's father died, his father's brothers would try to push aside their nephews. To prevent such a situation, another ritual was established. Sons were officially passed "into the hands" of their uncles, who had to give an oath that they would protect their nephews in the case of their brother's death. When this was done, the uncle was effectively a second father, and he was even called "father" by his nephew.

THE LAST WILL OF A KING

Princes often died in war or from disease. These deaths were often quick and unexpected. However, in those situations where a prince could predict his imminent death, he could do several things to try influence the fate of his lands and his immediate family.

An interesting story from the Chronicles: Prince Vladimir

Vasil'kovich, who was a famed builder of cities, became fatally ill. He had no heirs, only an adopted daughter, Iziaslava. He didn't like any of his other relatives, because they were friendly with the Tatars.

And so, Vladimir chose a single heir, his cousin, Mstislav Danilovich, after signing an accord that Mstislav would protect his family, and would marry Iziaslava only to a suitor of her choosing (very rare for that time!) Mstislav also began to treat Vladimir's wife, Olga, as his own mother.

For agreeing to do this, Mstislav was given all of Vladimir's lands, even though usually they were split among all the heirs. Surprisingly, no one disputed this inheritance, though that was probably because the Tatars approved.

Even though there were obviously many difficulties in the unsettled life of the Russian princes, many people were honorable and at least tried to live in a manner that would be worthy of their family, their city, and their faith.

CHAPTER 13
HOW THE TSARS USED TO
CELEBRATE CHRISTMAS

I've always loved good, old-fashioned pageantry. In my novels, I try to include moments of it, since it's not something authors nowadays tend to indulge in. But Medieval Russians really understood how to do pageantry well, especially on major feast days of the Church. Here is how the Tsars celebrated Christmas in the 16th and 17th centuries.

The celebration began early in the morning on Christmas Eve. The day began with the Tsar's "secret exit" from the palace. The Tsars of Moscow and all Rus loved to commemorate every great feast of the Church with generous acts of almsgiving. This was certainly true of Christmas.

All of Moscow—from the first among the rich to the last among the poor—prepared for the feast as they were able. That day, every single alleyway and public square in old Moscow was covered with beggars, even before the sun rose. Everyone hoped that the Tsar would see them and satisfy their hunger at least for the holy days.

In fact, the Tsar's "secret exit" was no secret at all. An action once performed as a pleasant surprise soon became a custom, and eventually it was written down as an official part of the Tsar's yearly business. If the Tsar couldn't come out to see the people, one of the more important boyars would do it as his representative. In any case, only illness would usually prevent the Tsar from fulfilling the duty himself.

Four hours before sunrise, the Russian autocrat would leave for his pious labor, dressed in the humble clothing of a simple boyar. The darkness of the winter night lay over snow-enveloped Moscow.

Before the Tsar walked a lantern-bearer. To either side of the Tsar walked members of the "Secret Department," followed by the Streltsy. Everyone the Tsar encountered received money.

The first place he visited was the Great Prison Court (Большой тюремный двор). The Tsar visited every prison cell and listened to the complaints of every single prisoner. Some he would pardon on the spot. Others would receive reduced sentences. Still others got a silver ruble and 50 kopecks for the feast. Then the Tsar would command a special feast for all the prisoners on the day of the feast.

After leaving the prisons, the Tsar walked through the "White City" and Kitai-Gorod. Every poor person he met received a personal gift of alms. After finishing his "secret walk," he would rest for a bit, change into his royal garments, and attend the Christmas Eve service at one of the house chapels of the royal palace.

The Tsar stood, surrounded by his boyars, representatives of the Duma, and other courtiers, listening to the Royal Hours before Vespers. For the vigil service, the Tsar wore a special white fur coat, fringed with hand-wrought lace-work and stitching of solid gold. In this coat, he walked into the Cathedral of the Dormition in the Kremlin, where he stood attending to the entire service, which included a special doxology for the Tsar, exclaimed by the archdeacon.

After this, the Patriarch (as described by the historian Zabelin), "with the authorities and the entire assembly greeted the Tsar." The Tsar officially congratulated the Patriarch and received his congratulations. Then, having received a blessing, he returned to the palace.

In the twilight hours, as everyone awaited the coming of the first star, the clergy of the Dormition Cathedral, along with the Tsar's Chosen Singers (an elite choir of 35 voices), came caroling to the royal palace. Sometimes, small ensembles from the Patriarchal, Metropolitan, or other local church choirs would join them.

The Tsar would greet the singers according to strict protocol, usually in the "Golden Room." By custom, he would give them both "white" and "red" honey in a golden and silver pot, respectively. Other than this traditional gift, each singer would also receive anything from eight 3-kopeck pieces to twelve rubles (a considerable sum for the time), depending on the "status" of the choir. Russian Tsars loved sacred chant, and so were especially generous to choir singers.

Then came the feast of the Nativity itself. For the traditional midnight service, the Tsar attended service at the "Golden Palace" house church. At ten in the morning, Moscow heard the first festal peal of the bells calling all faithful to the liturgy. Soon, the whole city would shake as all "forty forties" of Moscow's church bells rang.

By this time, the Tsar was in the "Stolovaia Room"—the most majestic of his rooms. He sat on his throne, next to which stood a special seat for the Patriarch. The boyars and the diaki (councilmen) sat on benches with velvet seats. All others stood.

After some time had passed, the Patriarch entered, preceded by the keepers of the Cathedral's keys (an official title of the Cathedral clergy) holding crosses and bearing holy water. An assembly of metropolitans, archbishops, bishops, archimandrites, and abbots accompanied the Patriarch. The Tsar stood at the Patriarch's entrance as he praised the birth of the Lord. After the customary series of hymns, the Patriarch personally greeted the "keeper of the Russian lands," and, after being invited, sat next to the Tsar.

After some time had passed, the Patriarch and his assembly went on to the palace of the queen. There, he greeted her and the entire family of the Tsar. All this while, the Tsar prepared for the liturgy in the Cathedral of the Dormition. At this liturgy, he bore his official regalia and dressed in his most festive "porphyry".

After liturgy, the Patriarch was invited back to the palace for lunch. Traditionally, the Tsar himself never sat down until he personally inspected the feast and made sure everything was done according to his command.

This personal command included tables set inside the palace for the poor and orphaned, of whom many hundreds would come every year for the feast. The tables included:

- Savory pies
- Baked goods
- Wooden jugs of kvass (Russian ale) and mead

At the command of an appointed boyar, doormen admitted the Tsar's guests and sat them at the tables. Each of them, from the name of the Tsar, received a small loaf of bread and a 50-kopeck piece. The appointed boyar would wait at the tables and ask the guests how they liked the food.

Only after the appointed boyar came to personally tell the Tsar that the guests were satisfied, given gifts, and sent away with a merciful word, did the Tsar himself sit in his throne room to feast with the great and powerful.

After this official feast was over, the Tsar gave himself to his family entirely.

Among the many other traditions during this culturally rich time, the third day of the feast is especially interesting. The Tsar would pick one of the local monasteries and travel there by sled. This sled was gilded and fantastically decorated.

The Tsar's seat was covered with Persian rugs. Two boyars and footmen attended the king in his sled.

The Tsar's retinue followed in a caravan of sleighs. No less than one hundred Streltsy guarded them. Uncounted multitudes of people surrounded the Tsar's sled. Many of them followed the "Tsar-father" on horseback, greeting the Tsar with loud cries. Having visited the holy places, the Tsar then always visited the grave of his parents, before returning to the palace.

That evening was a special party for the Tsar's family in the "Amusements Room" (Потешная палата). Musicians played the *gusli*, violins, organs, and cimbalom. Jesters and dwarfs amused the Tsar's family with songs, dances, and other entertainments. The first comedic plays in history were performed here (Alexei Mikhailovich was a great fan of theater).

Beginning with this private party, the feasting in the palace didn't end until the day before Theophany (January 5).

CHAPTER 14
MEDIEVAL MOSCOW

W ho lived in the Kremlin? Would you believe that in some parts of Moscow swearing (that is, using foul language) was prohibited by law? Where in Moscow did lions walk around (true story)? Here are some of the strangest facts about Medieval Moscow.

"KREMLINGRAD"—THE RESIDENTIAL CENTER OF THE CITY

Nowadays, we've become accustomed to think about the Kremlin as the seat and the personification of Russian power. Most of the buildings in today's Kremlin are either museums or actual government buildings. However, that was not always the case.

It's not by accident that in the Middle Ages foreigners called the Kremlin "Kremlingrad" (or "Kremlin the city"). In those times, the most important fort of the country was a kind of "city within the city." In fact, only a small part of it was dedicated to the Tsar's court. The greater part of the Kremlin (14-16th centuries) was filled with monasteries, churches, large houses belonging to important boyars, and even houses of guildsmen and clergy.

THE TSAR'S COURT WAS A PLACE FREE OF FOUL LANGUAGE AND WEAPONS

The heart of the Kremlin—the Tsar's court—was a holy place for the subjects of the Tsar. Therefore, special rules of behavior preserved the honor of the house of the ruler of Russia. Entrance into the court was strictly prohibited except for boyars, servants of the Tsar, or certain members of the clergy.

Boyars had to dismount from their horses or walk out of their sleds (in winter) at some distance before the entrance to the courtyard. Servants had to dismount even farther away than the boyars—at the square near the bell tower of Ivan the Great (III). Within the courtyard, no foul language was allowed. All weapons were to be left outside the courtyard. If someone were to accidentally bring in so much as a dagger, he would be immediately arrested and probably tortured as a suspected conspirator against the Tsar's life.

THE LOUD SQUARE

There's a saying in Russian – "to scream over all Ivanovksoe". It's not exactly a subtle phrase, but interestingly enough it came from a geographical section of Medieval Moscow.

The Tsar's peace and quiet was strictly guarded within his court. Meanwhile, only a few hundred steps away, the Square of Ivan was loud and full of people. In the 14-17th centuries, the square next to the bell tower of Ivan the Great had a complex of various government buildings. Here, from morning to night, people came with their various needs and complaints. Not only that, but in front of the main building, various corporal punishments were administered almost daily.

The most common form of corporal punishment was beating with rods. The screams and moans of the criminals filled the square until the moment of the day when the priests offered the Bloodless Sacrifice at the liturgy. This moment was always preceded by a special peal of the bells, and all corporal punishment ceased until the end of the liturgy. In early Medieval Moscow, the Tsar's decrees would also be publicly decried by a sexton. This is the source of the Russian phrase "to scream over all Ivanovskoe".

THE LION GATES—THE TSAR'S PERSONAL ZOO UNDER THE WALLS OF THE KREMLIN

In the beginning of the 16th century, a moat filled with water separated the walls of the Kremlin from the expansive marketplaces in the Red Square. Ivan the Terrible had the moat drained. In the space next to the Arsenal Tower, he and his successors kept lions and other exotic animals (gifts by emissaries from foreign countries).

Therefore, the adjoining gates to Kitai-Gorod ("China-town") were called "the lion gates." Today, they're known as the "Iveron Gates," named for a 17th century chapel which contained a copy of the Iveron Icon of the Mother of God from Athos. They are also known as the "Resurrection Gates," because in 1689 an icon of the Resurrection of Christ was hung on the main tower of the gates.

CROSSROADS "BELONGED" TO THE POOR

All crossroads in Moscow, which were called "little crosses" in older times, were often centers of public life. The most famous of these were:

- the "little cross of St. Nicholas," the intersection between Nikolskaia and Bogoiavlenskaia Streets

- the "little cross of the Saviour," at the Spasskie
  Gates of the Kremlin

Here, from the early morning, an "assembly" of the lower classes gathered. These included:

- minor merchants with various wares to hawk (from hand-written books to pancakes and kvass)
- clergy with no place to serve
- workers waiting to be hired
- the poor, maimed, and the fools for Christ

Completing this chaotic picture were the inhabitants of local poorhouses who asked for alms. Sometimes these professional beggars would include "props" to more effectively move the passers-by. One of these could be baskets with babies that were left at the doors of the poorhouse by starving mothers. But the most effective was an open casket with the dead body of a wanderer who had no money for a proper burial.

Whatever medieval Moscow was, it was certainly not boring!

CHAPTER 15

RUSSIAN WINTER

A s I mentioned in an earlier chapter, Russians, oddly enough, prefer to get married in the beginning of winter, on October 1 (October 14 by today's calendar), the Feast of the Protection. But Russians didn't just get married on this day. There were many folk traditions and beliefs associated with October 1, the traditional first day of winter. Here are five of the most interesting ones.

THE PILGRIM SONGS OF THE PROTECTION

As the first snow covers the land, people in the faraway reaches of Russia started to hear the half-liturgical, half-folk songs of wandering pilgrims. Their songs concerned events actually connected to the historical feast of the Protection. (For those who don't know, the feast is a commemoration of the miraculous deliverance of Constantinople from a barbarian horde in the 9th century). Here's one of these songs, in my very rough translation:

> *The enemies came to the Kingdom of the Greeks,*
> *They threatened them with war and destruction.*

The song goes on to describe how the surrounded Greeks, inspired to repentant prayer, came to the church to ask for help. The prayer reached the ears of the Mother of God, who came down personally from Heaven. All the shocked people turned to the Mediatress of the human race and cried out to her: "Why have you come down yourself to us, you dove, you all-pure, all-gracious one? Has brilliant heaven become bitter with our sins? Have you come down from the Creator to punish us?"

But She answers thus:

> *For me heaven has lost its joy,*
> *The firmament's light has darkened.*
> *For every hour the angels bring to me*
> *Bitter tears of Christians.*
> *How disturbed I become, how sorrowful!*
> *So I came to you directly to give comfort,*
> *To pray with you together to the Lord...*

PAGAN ECHOES

The people's imagination often combined the Protection of the Mother of God with the fairy tale of "the virgin Sun bearing a spotless sheet." The sheet is a personification of the dawn and the twilight. According to the folk storytellers, the sun spins this sheet from silver and gold thread that come down from the sky:

> *On the sea, on the ocean,*
> *On the Island of Buyan,*
> *Lies a stone, white as snow.*
> *On this stone a table stands,*
> *And on this table sits a maiden.*
> *But she is not a maiden fair,*
> *She is the All Pure Mother, the Mother of God...*

The image of the Mother of God on the stone is interesting, considering the Christian interpretation of one of the prophecies of Daniel (the stone cut out of the mountain without human hands). The stone, according to the liturgical tradition of the Orthodox Church, symbolizes the ever-virginity of the Mother of God.

The people used to pray to the goddess Dawn for protection, but Christianity changed the image of this goddess and transformed it into the face of Mary. A new version of the prayer might sound like this:

> *O beautiful maiden of the dawn,*
> *Mother, all pure Mother of God!*
> *Cover my sorrows and sicknesses with your veil!*
> *Cover me with your protection from spirits dark!*
> *Your veil is as strong as the stone of Alatyr! (a*
> *   legendary stone where pagan sacrifices were*
> *   offered)*

THE FOLK VERSION OF THE CHRISTIAN FEAST

The newly converted Slavs changed the actual historical event celebrated on October 1 into an entirely different tale.

In the old times, the people used to say, the Mother of God was a pilgrim who wandered over the earth. She happened to enter into a certain village where all the people had long forgotten God and the works of mercy. She asked for shelter. But everywhere she heard the same answer: "We don't take in wanderers!"

At that moment, Elijah the prophet was flying by on his fiery chariot, and he heard these terrible words. He could not bear to hear such insults uttered against the holy lady, and he began to hurl down his thunderbolts and to pour down heavy rain that threatened to destroy the entire village.

The people were afraid and began to cry out. The Mother

of God felt sorry for them. She covered them with her veil, and saved the same people who had insulted and wounded her. Her kindness melted their hearts, and from that moment they became the most hospitable of villages.

THE DEPARTURE OF THE BIRDS

Just as the arrival of the birds in March/April heralded the beginning of spring, the last cranes left for the south (traditionally) on the Protection. If they left on this day, it's a good sign. If they left earlier, it meant the winter was going to be a howler.

PREPARATIONS FOR WINTER

The Protection is the time to prepare the house for winter. Every good husband takes care to prepare the stores of wood, to clean the stove. "Catch the warmth before Protection," the saying goes, "or your house just won't be the same!"

On the eve of the Protection, the dirty straw beds of winter must be burned. This action, for the superstitious peasant, was a kind of warding against the evil eye. Old ladies also burned their bark-shoes, hoping to "warm up their feet to walk faster" for winter. Children were prepared against winter colds by being doused with cold water on the porch.

Even the spirits of the forests, the *leshye*, stopped walking about after the first day of winter. But they didn't go down without a fight. The folk tales told how the *leshye* would break trees, uproot bushes, send wild animals out of their holes, until the earth swallowed them up again until spring. With the melting of the rivers, they'd be sure to come back to do their usual mischief. But the winter was a time of rest for all.

CHAPTER 16

CHRISTMAS TRADITIONS OF
OLD RUS

A few years ago, while spending a very illuminating six months in Belarus, my wife and I were invited to a local television program to discuss family Christmas traditions.

I was pleasantly surprised by how many of my wife's family's traditions were similar to our own, even though my family emigrated in the early 20th century. It turns out that Christmas traditions are among the best preserved among all old Russian traditions.

THE MANY MEANINGS OF THE WORD "CAROL"

"Koliada was born on the night before Christmas..."

The Russian word for "carol"—"koliada"—is a strange word, even in Russian. Historians still can't agree about its meaning. Even folk traditions can't agree, giving the term all kinds of different meanings.

In North Russia, for example, "koliada" is the name for the eve of Christmas. "Caroling," in this sense, means celebrating the day by visiting all the houses in a village with congratulations and songs. This procession is always led by a makeshift "star of Bethlehem." In the Novgorod region, on the other hand, "koliada" refers to the presents that the carolers receive during these visits.

In southern and western regions, "koliada" is synonymous with Christmas itself and even the entire 12 days afterward. As for Belarus, "koliadovat'" (caroling) traditionally means "to praise Christ". But in Smolensk (not far from Belarus), it means "to ask alms," thereby losing its original meaning completely.

In ancient times, all Russians caroled on Christmas Eve. But the caroling tradition only survived in Ukraine and Belarus. Traditionally, the young people of the village, after the end of the long church service, would walk in a large crowd from window to window, staying longer near houses where there was a fire.

Generous hosts would "festoon" the carolers with sausages, small pancakes, nuts, or even money. In the regions of Kiev and Volhynia, all the gathered money was all given back to the church. In other places, the money went to a special village-wide Christmas feast.

Even nowadays, Ukrainian carols are the most varied and ancient of all east Slavic carols. Here's an example of one of the oldest, with some unusual lyrics:

> *On the blue sea*
> *There's a ship on the water,*
> *In that ship*
> *There are three gates.*
> *In the first gate,*
> *The moon shines.*
> *In the second, the sun sets.*
> *In the third, the Lord Himself walks.*
> *He takes the keys,*
> *And opens Heaven.*

CHILDREN'S CAROLS

In Russia, few regions preserved their ancient caroling traditions. Most of the time, only children's carols survived. Even at the beginning of the 20th century, you could see crowds of children in certain villages. They would always follow a boy carrying a lantern made in the form of a star. All the others followed him, running from house to house, wherever people let them in.

> *Koliada, koliada!*
> *Koliada has come*
> *On the eve of Christmas.*
> *We went, we sought*
> *Holy Koliada*
> *In every yard,*
> *Every alleyway.*
> *We found Koliada*
> *In Peter's yard,*
> *There's an iron fence,*
> *Inside the yard, the towers stand.*
> *In the first tower is the moon so bright,*
> *In the second—the brilliant sun,*
> *In the third—a myriad of stars...*

This carol continues by praising the master of the house, who is called "the bright moon," while his wife is called "the brilliant sun," and their many children "the myriad of stars." Finally, the carol ends with:

> *Greetings, master and mistress,*
> *For many ages, many years!"*
> *Sometimes, the ending is even more expressive:*
> *The master in his house is like Adam in Paradise,*

The mistress in the house is like a pancake in honey,
The little children are like the red-green grapes.

Finally, the "star-bearer" bows and greets the master and mistress in regular speech.

HOW UKRAINIANS USED TO GREET THE COMING LORD

The rites still practiced in some Ukrainian villages are reminiscent of the rites of ancient Rus. As soon as the first star lights the night sky (called the "star of Bethlehem"), the elder of any house brings a batch of hay into the house and lays it down at the main icon corner, then covers it with a clean sheet. Then a new sheaf of wheat or rye is placed on top of it.

The traditional meal for the evening—"kutia," boiled wheat with honey—is also placed under the icons, along with a special compote of boiled pears, plums, and other fruits. Then, the dinner can begin. Dinner is set on a white tablecloth, and everyone in the house sits down. All the food is Lenten, and the kutia and compote are eaten last.

During dinner, the women read the fortunes of the coming harvest. This is done by picking out the first bit of hay that comes out from underneath the tablecloth. If it's a long piece, the harvest will be good. Then they take out a single straw from the sheaf that sits under the icons. If a full head of wheat comes out, then the harvest will be successful. If the straw is just a straw, then there will be famine.

When everyone has eaten and the mistress of the house begins to clear away the food, the fortune-telling continues. This time, the table is strewn with hay. If there are more black straws than yellow and red, then the rye harvest will be good. If there are more red and yellow than black, then there will be a good harvest of oats and wheat.

The sheaf of wheat stays under the icons until the New Year. From the "holy night" (December 24) until January 1, no self-respecting mistress of the house will sweep away any dirt from the house. After the new year, they gather everything and burn it in the yard. This is for good luck, because it is supposed to protect the harvest and the vegetable garden from pests.

CHRIST WALKS THE EARTH ON CHRISTMAS EVE

There's an ancient tradition that on midnight of Christmas Eve, the gates of Heaven open up, and the Son of God descends from the Heights to earth. "All-brilliant paradise" is visible to righteous people during this time, revealing all its treasures and mysteries.

All the waters of Paradise's rivers come alive and begin to move. All sources on earth turn into wine and are given miraculous healing power. In the gardens of Paradise, the trees suddenly blossom and golden apples ripen on the branches. And from the depths of Paradise, the sun spreads its generous gifts to the land that is covered in snow. As the people say,

"If anyone will pray exactly at midnight, everything he asks will be given. Everything will be as it is written."

There's a Serbian custom to come outside at midnight and stand in an open field or at a crossroads and look at the sky. According to the words of the elders, God reveals the beauties of heaven to the righteous. They see how the golden Dawn leads out the sun from the depths of Paradise's gardens. As the sun passes, it sprinkles Paradise with gold and roses.

THE HOLY DAYS

The period after Christmas and before Theophany (January 6) is called "Sviatki," the holy days. Ancient traditions of Rus were preserved best in these days surrounding Christmas.

The Holy Days are days of singing and feasting. It's a time for which the rich imagination of folk beliefs and traditions were created. In the midst of the most difficult time of the year for the working man, the Russian folk seem to awaken from hibernation and boldly feast day and night, singing and dancing as though they have limitless energy.

CHAPTER 17
RUSSIA'S GROUNDHOG DAY

Did you know that Groundhog Day is also a Russian holiday? Well, not exactly, but February 2 is also when Russians "check for winter's end." I don't think this is anything but coincidence, but the feast of the Meeting of the Lord falls on February 2, and in the conception of the Russian folk, this was the day that winter first receives notice that its days are numbered.

OLD WOMAN WINTER VS. YOUNG WOMAN SPRING

The freezing temperatures that often occur around the feast of the Meeting of the Lord (February 2) remind the peasant folk of Russia that winter doesn't want to give in to spring. At the same time, it's no surprise that the common folk consider the Meeting to be the last "meeting" between winter and spring in their battle.

On this day, according to folk beliefs, winter fights a final, desperate battle against sunny spring. After this day, Old Woman-Winter runs away, hurries, avoids even glancing at the fiery eyes of her antagonist-spring, who gets stronger by the day. Old Woman-Winter feels that the streets that she's just covered with snow will soon be covered by the feet of people celebrating a new feast—the birth of spring.

In some places, this old song is still sung in the first days of February, especially by children:

> *Here comes the month that warms my sides*
> *For a long time the earth's been cold,*
> *But now the cow's sides get red with warmth*
> *And the cow's, and the horse's*
> *And the white-haired old man's too!*
> *Good old Frost, the son of Frost!*
> *Don't be grumpy, Old Man Winter,*
> *Run away from our village,*
> *Beyond the thrice-nine lands,*
> *Beyond the thrice-ten seas!*
> *There your own estates await,*
> *They've been abandoned far too long,*
> *Overcome in powdered snow,*
> *Locked behind seven seals of ice,*
> *Seven locks of metal,*
> *Seven heavy bolts!*

GUESSING WINTER'S END

All the older members of any village community know that if the eve of the Meeting of the Lord is clear, if the sky is filled with stars, then winter's time "to weep" won't begin for a while yet. Spring will be late this year, they say.

But this is only one of many folk beliefs that surround winter's end. Most of them have to do with February 2 itself. For example, in the Tula region, it's considered bad luck to travel far on sleds on February 2. You shouldn't trust winter any more. If the day is especially warm, it's considered to be a sign that the winter is going to be a rotten one (i.e. bring a lot of disease with it).

In Kostroma, the locals don't quite agree with their Tula counterparts. They say that if on the Meeting of the Lord, "the walls are wet from sparrows," that only means that spring is coming early, but not that it's going to be pestilent. In Ryazan', it's said that if there's snow on February 2, then it's going to be a wet spring. If it's a snowstorm, then they say that "the Meeting will pick up all the feed." In other words, it'll be a long summer with a short harvest season, and the animals won't have enough food for the following winter.

A CAUTIONARY WINTER'S TALE

In the Kashyrsk region, an interesting story was often repeated in the local villages in the early 19th century. It was used to prove the folk belief that you shouldn't travel far on February 2.

"Once upon a time," they said, "there was an old man with his family. They lived well and ate well. He had a lot of everything, and the Lord gifted him with smart and talented children. Whatever the old man couldn't think up himself, his children invented. And if they didn't know something, the old man always taught them.

"The old man organized to have all his kids married on the same day. He thought it would be a good idea to feed all his in-laws, and so he prepared for them a mighty feast for Maslenitsa Week before Lent. So he thought it would be a good idea to travel far in search of fish, to make a buck or two, and to make his guests even happier.

"But he kept putting it off, waiting for good traveling weather. And—lo and behold!—it's already the Meeting of the Lord, and Maslenitsa soon after that! So the old man took his whole family, save the old ladies and the kids, and filled seven train compartment with his goods.

"But as soon as the old ladies heard about it, they had a bad feeling. They moaned and cried to their husbands. 'Don't go!'

they said. But the men paid no heed. 'They're making it up,' said the men. Always having bad dreams, always depressed. It's the domovoi (house imp) that's pushing them to this silliness. Don't argue with the old women, that's true enough! But don't listen to them either!'

"No, thought the old man. I'm going to go get my fish. I want to feed my in-laws proper this Maslenitsa.

"What can you do with a muzhik? He's stubborn as an ox and has never listened to anyone! It was an ominous, warm day, that Meeting of the Lord. The old women moaned even louder, understanding the evil omen. 'Look!' they said. 'Look outside, my dear one! It's so warm! The freeze is over. Spring is coming. Nothing good can come of this!'

"But the old man still went. Seven compartments full of goods and sons left that morning. The old women waited for their men for a week, but not a word! They waited for a second week, and still no news. Another week's gone by, and still their beloved haven't returned! It's already Meatfare Day, and then came the rumors. An old man drowned over there somewhere...

"The old women wailed louder than before. Everyone's celebrating Cheesefare, but for the old women it's already Lent! And then they heard. Their husbands fell into the cracking ice on the Volga together with all their goods. No one survived...

"But why are you surprised? Everyone knows that only bad things happen to those who don't listen to the old beliefs and the old people's wisdom!"

CALLING THE SUN

By the evening of the feast of the Meeting of the Lord, not long before twilight, all the children gather together to listen to the tales told by the elders. Then they get together on a high hilltop and begin to call to the sun, asking it to show itself "from behind the hills." If it does, it shows them that winter did indeed have its proper meeting with spring.

Here are the words to one of these songs that called to the sun:

> *O you bright sun,*
> *Come, peek out*
> *From behind the hills!*
> *Look out, my sun,*
> *Until the time of spring!*
> *Have you seen, my sun*
> *The beautiful spring?*
> *Have you met, my sun,*
> *Your sister-true?*
> *Have you seen, my sun,*
> *Old Yaga?*
> *Baba Yaga?*
> *Old Woman-Winter?*
> *Have you seen how she*
> *Ran away from spring*
> *From the Beautiful One?*
> *Has she carried the frost away in a bag?*
> *Did she shake the cold over the land?*
> *Did she run away,*
> *Hiding under the mountain?*
> *Did she meet the spring,*
> *The beautiful sister of the sun?*

If the sun did in fact "peek out" before sunset from "behind the hills," then the joyful crowd of children ran back to the village with the news that the last freeze had passed. But if the sun didn't come out, then there'd be another wave of sub-zero temperatures around the 11th of February.

PRACTICAL MATTERS

Other than the mystical moments surrounding February 2, the traditional warming during this time is a reminder to the responsible head of household. It's time to begin fixing the summer harnesses—both for riding and for work in the field. There's even a special day dedicated to this work. February 3 is known among the peasants as "Fixing Day."

On this day, the men got up before dawn to see to the horses—did the *Domovoi* mess with them at all on the previous night? This is connected with a superstition that if the house imp is somehow unhappy, he chooses the night of February 2-3 to "ride the horses all night." So the usual "offering" to the *Domovoi* is even more extravagant than usual—a special pot of porridge set apart by a ring of burning coals.

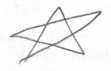

CHAPTER 18
RUSSIAN MARDI GRAS

Russians generally have a bad reputation as being dour and grumpy. Some Russians will even agree with this characterization, making a point to ridicule how Americans always smile. But there are a few weeks in the year when no Russian will pretend to be anything but joyful. One of these is, obviously, Easter Week. But another almost equally festal week is the week before Lent, called Maslenitsa.

MASLENITSA: THE MEANING, HISTORY, AND TRADITIONS OF "RUSSIAN MARDI GRAS"

The last day of the week before Lent is called "Forgiveness Sunday." It's a fitting end to the series of preparatory weeks before Lent. This "introduction" to the Fast lasts 22 days, and during this time, the Church "gives the tone" for the faithful's entry into a different spiritual space.

This far-sighted attention to Lent is completely justified, because Great Lent is the heart of the entire liturgical year in most Christian churches. Lent is a special time. As the poet Natalia Karpova said, it's "seven slow weeks, given to you for repentance." The rhythm of life changes. Naturally, radical changes in the soul don't occur in an hour, and so a serious preparation of the mind, the emotions, and the body is necessary.

If we study the history of this week, we find out that the preparatory rhythms of "Cheesefare Week," as it's also called, are among the oldest traditions in the Christian Church. They appeared thanks to the influence of the Palestinian monastic tradition. Palestinian monks spent nearly the entire 40 days of the Fast completely alone in the desert. By the last week of the fasting period, Holy Week, they returned to the monastery, but not all of them. Some of them would have died in the desert.

Since the monks understood that every new Lent could be their last, they asked forgiveness of each other on the Sunday before. This is where "forgiveness Sunday" comes from.

This week's special allowance to eat dairy on Wednesday and Friday is also of monastic provenance. After all, what is the desert? It's a lack of food, and sometimes, even water. Naturally, the monks needed to gather physical strength before embarking on this labor. The monks didn't eat meat (they never ate meat), so this week was essentially fast-free for them.

Laypeople assumed this monastic tradition, and the meaning changed somewhat. After all, laypeople don't go into the desert, so they have no especial need to load up on proteins. For laypeople, this week's feasting has a different focus. The world has many temptations, and abandoning all of them suddenly can be dangerous. Therefore, the limitations of the Fast are introduced slowly. This week, for example, meat is no longer allowed, and neither are weddings, interestingly enough. However, joyful feasting is definitely the order of the day, provided it's still moderated somewhat. After all, Lent is at the doorstep.

THE PRE-CHRISTIAN HISTORY OF MASLENITSA

Maslenitsa is actually an old pagan holiday known in Rus even before the coming of Christianity. It must immediately be said that the Church has never considered Maslenitsa to be part of its tradition, and there is no feast in the Church calendar called Maslenitsa. "Cheesefare Week" only happens to coincide with it.

However, in a certain sense, Christianity has never been intolerant of paganism. On the contrary, the Church often "baptized" traditional pagan holidays and feasts, infusing them with new meaning, thereby making the cultural transition from pagan to Christian more organic.

So if the Church didn't make Maslenitsa part of the Church calendar, it did denude it of its sacred character. Instead, it made this vivid and even grotesque period into a week of rest, relaxation, and feasting.

THE MEANING OF PAGAN MASLENITSA

We can start with the fact that in ancient times this holiday was far more multi-faceted than in the centuries immediately preceding the Revolution. At its heart lies an idea common to all pagan religions: the cult of the "cycle of time." The older the civilization, the more it tends to accent this idea of time's repetitiveness.

Ancient Slavic Maslenitsa was celebrated in early spring, when the day began to win its battle against the long night. This would be around March 21 or 22 according to our calendar. In old Rus, the first days of spring's first month were always unpredictable. Warm weather could quickly be replaced by harsh frost, and vice versa. Spring battles with winter. Maslenitsa celebrates this final crossing from cold to warm, after which the spring triumphs over the winter. Life will soon again follow its more predictable rhythms.

Naturally, the coming spring was connected with fertility cults. The land resurrects, having absorbed the last of the winter's snows, filling itself with "seed." And now, people had to help mother Earth, to give the natural process a touch of the sacred.

Speaking more prosaically, the rites of Maslenitsa consecrate the earth, filling it with power to give abundant harvest. For peasants, the backbone of old Russian society, a good harvest is the only true wealth, so these rites were naturally important. In that sense, Maslenitsa was a kind of "pagan liturgy," the peasants bringing an offering to nature and its elements instead of God.

Not only the land, but the peasants themselves receive the blessing of fertility for taking part in Maslenitsa. If you eat the food given by Mother-Earth, then you will also give life to another. The circle of life, the natural cycle of life and death and rebirth, were central to the pagan mindset. Life itself was the most important value, and everything else was a means to attaining it. That's also why there was an element of ancestor worship in the early Maslenitsa celebrations.

After Christianity, the sacred meaning of Maslenitsa practically disappeared, leaving behind only its external trappings and slightly manic joy.

THE FEAST OF KOLODII

An even older name for Maslenitsa is Kolodii. This is connected with a bizarre ritual that survived even to recent times in Ukraine and Belarus. During this entire week, in addition to the other rites associated with the week, the villagers celebrated "the life of the koloda." They took a thick stick (a "koloda") and dressed it as a human being. On Monday, the koloda "was born," on Tuesday, it was "baptized," on Wednesday it lived all the difficult moments of its life. On Thursday, it "died," on Friday it was "buried," and on Saturday, everyone "mourned it." On Sunday was the culmination of Kolodii.

During this whole week, the women carried it around the village and tied it to all who were unmarried. This included those who had illegitimate children. Of course, no one wanted to be branded with this label, so the women-bearers had to be bought off. Colored ribbon, beads, plates, drinks, or sweets were considered appropriate.

THE BLIN

The food most associated with Maslenitsa is the thick pancake, the *blin*, that is still consumed in obscene amounts in any self-respecting Russian household. The famous Russian folklorist Afanasiev believed the *blin* to be a symbol of the sun, connecting the meal to the fertility rites of reborn spring. However, another possibility is that the *blin* is the ancient food-offering for dead ancestors, having a profound symbolic meaning.

It has a circular shape (a hint of eternity). It's warm (reminding of earthly joy) and made from wheat, water, and milk (the elements of life). A custom that survived long into the 19th century testifies to the probability of this second hypothesis. On the first day of Maslenitsa, a few *blini* were left in the attic "to feed the departed" or given directly to the local poor, so that they would pray for the family's departed relatives. Thus, it is still said, "The first *blin* is for remembrance."

Some of the other ancient traditions of Maslenitsa week were also associated with the commemoration of the departed. One of these was the famous fist-fight so well depicted in Nikita Mikhalkov's Oscar-winning film "The Siberian Barber."

These fights were quite dangerous. Sometimes people would die, harking back to ancient times when such fights were part of a sacrifice to Mother-Earth. The blood of fallen warriors was always the best offering to the gods.

The last victim of Maslenitsa was not human, however. An effigy of winter was triumphantly burned at the end of the week, and the ashes were scattered over the field. This was the final consecration of the soil, often accompanied by songs that would call the earth to bring forth abundant fruit in the coming year.

CHAPTER 19   ·
TO CELEBRATE THE COMING
OF SPRING

Afrequent writer's trick is using the time of the year as a contrast or complement to his characters' inner journeys. In my first novel, the change of season from fall to winter mirrors the development of the characters. But I didn't want the coming of spring in the second novel to be too obvious. One of the main characters is suffering through a personal loss, a death, on several levels. I needed to find some aspect of the coming of spring that would work as a good foil for his inner state.

In my research, I found several folk traditions associated with the Orthodox springtime feast of Annunciation. Naturally, a late winter-early spring church holiday would be associated with the coming of spring. Russians always met the bright holiday of Annunciation with cleanliness and good order. On this day, the Orthodox Church remembers the good news given by the Archangel Gabriel to the Virgin Mary concerning the birth of the Lord Jesus Christ. Here are seven ways in which Russians traditionally (in more or less pagan-inflected ways) celebrated the feast.

OUT WITH THE OLD!

On the eve of Annunciation, the superstitious peasant, in preparation for the feast, would burn his straw bedroll, which would have become disgusting over the course of the winter. Then all the winter clothes would be smoked out, and sometimes the whole house. Thus all the "evil spirits," birthed by the dark powers of Morana, the goddess of winter and death, would be banished in preparation for the coming of Spring the Beautiful. This was also the time to burn all clothing of people who had been seriously ill, to protect them from any dark magic.

"THE BIRD DOES NOT WEAVE ITS NEST; THE MAID DOES NOT PLAIT HER HAIR."

In Russian folk consciousness, Annunciation was associated with the spring awakening of nature. To this day, many Russians, superstitious or not, will not do any physical work. In older times, peasants were forbidden from working the ground, because this was the time that the earth "opened up," releasing to the surface all the snakes, mice, and insects that had been sleeping all winter. It was said, "If a bird weaves its nest on Annunciation, its wings will grow weak; never will it fly, but will live out its days by walking on the ground."

"AS SOON AS THE BIRDS ARRIVE, THE WARMTH WILL COME BACK"

The beginning of spring was associated with the return of migrating birds, and it was considered that the birds literally brought back the warmth. So to make spring come faster, people imitated the flight of birds. One way this was done was to bake small breads in the shape of birds in flight (though this was associated not so much with Annunciation, but with the celebration of the 40 martyrs of Sebaste two weeks earlier, but the principle is the same).

Children and young people took these "zhavoronky" to elevated places—roofs, hills, trees—and left them there. Sometimes, the breads were tied to stakes in the garden, and the wind rocked them back and forth, making it look like they were flying. Sometimes they would be eaten that same day, sometimes left for the next year. If so, they would be left in houses and gardens—anywhere, really, in the hope that they would bring good luck.

"PAY TO FREE THE BIRDS, AND THE BIRDS WILL PRAY FOR YOU TO GOD"

From time immemorial in Rus there was a custom on Annunciation to free birds from cages. In the cities, poor people caught birds in advance, brining them by the hundreds to the public markets. They always asked for a little money before releasing them. Merchants and shoppers, hearing the voices of the bird-catchers, were lavish in their payment to release the birds. By doing this, they hastened the coming of warmth and spring, and the end of winter. They were, in essence, bringing a kind of sacrifice to mother nature.

CALLING THE FIRST SPRING RAIN

On this day, the children of the village began to call for the first spring rain. From earliest morning, everyone watched for the coming of the first cloud. As soon as the sky darkened even a little, the children sang this song:

> *Rain, rain!*
> *Adorn yourself to be seen.*
> *Pour down, rain,*
> *On grandmother's rye,*

On grandfather's wheat,
Pour buckets down on the young girl's flax.
Hurry, hurry, rain!
Hurry quickly, come strongly,
And make us warm!

If the rain did come as called, everyone tried to get as wet as possible. It was supposed to bring good luck.

CALLING FOR SPRING

While the children sang their childish songs, young men and women did the more important work of "calling for spring." After lunch, they would take pies that they had baked in the morning, find a place under the open sky, face the East, say a prayer. Then someone would call out, "Bless us, O God, to begin calling for spring!" And all of those who had assembled would begin to sing the traditional song. They would sing it while sitting in a circle, eating, drinking, and having a good time. Then they would get up and dance in the circle and sometimes even pair off in dance.

Here is one version of that traditional song:

We greet you, O sun most beautiful!
Rejoice, our beautiful sun!
Roll, roll out from behind the mountain,
Rise up above the bright world,
Cover the grass, the blue flowers,
The bluebells with your eyes, your rays.
Warm my girl's heart with your gentle caress,
Look into the heart of the brave youths,
Take out the evil spirits from their souls,
Pour into them your living water,
Whose source is locked, and the key is in Dawn's hands.
Dawn the bright took a walk and lost the keys.

And I (name) walked along the road and found it.
I will love him whom I will, and I lock my heart
For him whom I choose. I lock my heart for you,
(name), for many years, for the long springs,
for the endless ages by a secret, unbreakable mystery.
Amen!

FROM THE HUT TO THE UPPER ROOM

With the coming of the Annunciation, young married couples left the main room of the hut for a smaller room. Unheated by the stove, it was almost like a porch. The small children and the older people remained in the hut. Basically all the work was now moved outdoors. Thus, Annunciation declared the end of winter work and the beginning of the work on the fields.

CHAPTER 20

HOW RUSSIANS GIVE JOY TO THEIR DEAD

As much as my novels are traditional historical fantasies set in a mythical early Rus, the events and characters are equally inspired by the last days of Tsarist Russia. That time period was full of contradictions (much like modern Russia, actually). A revival of traditional monasticism was paralleled by a growth in Spiritism. The gap between the elites and everyone else grew by the hour, not by the day. Literary feuds between Slavophiles and Westernizers were moments of national importance.

This tension between tradition and innovation is also a central theme of my first novel, *The Song of the Sirin.* One way this tension is expressed is through the preservation of ancient traditions concerning respect for dead ancestors. In Vasyllia (the central setting of my novel), the rich have largely lost all traditions connected with remembrance of ancestors. The poor, on the contrary, have preserved many of them.

Although the novel takes some creative liberties, I've borrowed from historical Russian traditions surrounding the commemoration of the dead around Easter time.

RADONITSA (THE TIME OF JOY)

On the second Tuesday after Pascha (Easter), everyone rushes to the cemeteries to congratulate the dead with the risen Christ who defeated the power of death. Here's one of the many songs sung on the occasion, this one by religious pilgrims:

> *Let us sing a joyous song today*
> *Christ is risen from the tomb*
> *God has risen from the dead, He who is alive from the*
> *ages,*
> *And He gave life to man who is dead in the world.*
> *For today we rejoice in song,*
> *Today we celebrate with our souls and bodies,*
> *Kissing each other on the cheeks,*
> *We forgive each other's sins...*

Pagan Russians imagined the land of the dead as being inside the earth. Those pagan attitudes didn't really disappear, even after Christianity. People believed that as Mother Earth began to weep spring tears of joy, her loving heart awakened after winter. As a result, the inhabitants of the land of the dead breathed easier.

The coming of springtime, the rebirth of nature, and the joy of the dead after winter were all connected. Everyone feels the joy of Pascha.

WEDDINGS

Even though these days are associated with commemoration of the dead, they are also a time for weddings. Some girls awaited this time with just as much excitement as for Pascha itself. According to Church practice, the first day you can get married after the long period of Lent is on Thomas Sunday (the first Sunday after Pascha). During this entire week, it was traditional to give gifts to the newly-married:

> *I will come, I will come*
> *I will come to the King's City,*
> *I will beat down, I will beat down,*
> *With my spears the city's wall!*
> *I will roll out, I will roll out*
> *The barrels from the treasury.*
> *I will gift, I will gift*
> *Them to my father-in-law.*
> *Be kind to me, be kind to me,*
> *Like my own dear father!*
> *I will come, I will come,*
> *I will come to the King's City!*
> *I will beat down, I will beat down,*
> *With my spears the city's wall!*
> *I will carry out, I will carry out,*
> *I will carry out a fox's pelt.*
> *I will gift, I will gift,*
> *I will gift it to my mother-in-law.*
> *Be kind to me, be kind to me,*
> *Like my own dear mother!"*

This curious song probably dates back as far as the 11th century, when the Rus still made regular raids on the "King's City," that is, Constantinople.

THE RED HILL

The first day of the commemoration of the dead, Thomas Sunday, is also called "krasnaia gorka" (the red hill). This name is ancient. Hills, in the Slavic pagan imagination, are the birthplaces of the gods and mankind. All Slavs used to worship mountains and always performed their sacrifices in high places.

The other meaning of the word "red" (krasny) is "beautiful." Therefore, the first festival of resurrected spring is rightly called "the beautiful hill."

In pagan times, this day was celebrated by lighting sacred fires on hilltops in honor of the god Dazhdbog. Various sacrifices were performed here, and this was also the time to settle grievances (a kind of "folk court"). When Christianity took down the idols that used to decorate the tops of these hills and replaced them with churches, it "sanctified" the red hills and made them eternally beautiful.

In pagan times, the day after the sacrificial fires was the time to celebrate the dead by feasting in their honor. This tradition continued, in a modified form, after Russia's Christianization. Today, the main day of celebrating the dead is on Tuesday, not Monday.

Wednesdays of this week were the days that pagan Russians got married. The pagan priests would bless the couples on the "red hills." The rest of the week was dedicated to feasting in honor of the newly-married couples. The loudest singing, the most boisterous dancing, was reserved for Saturday of Thomas week.

GIVING JOY TO THE DEAD

While the young people dance and sing, an entirely different set of rites is performed in the cemeteries. From Thomas Sunday on, the dead are "given joy" by the living. First all mothers who lost their children, all wives who lost their husbands, all orphans who lost their parents come and begin their ritual lamentation.

Leftovers from the Paschal feast are placed on all the gravesites. From this day on, the cemeteries are filled with feasting people.Honey and mead are poured over the gravesites "to treat the souls of our fathers." In Belarussian villages, even until the early 20th century, people feasted on tables that were physically placed over the gravesites of their parents. This harks back to the ancient pagan *trizna*, the ritual feast on the mound of fallen warriors after a battle.

After everyone is done feasting, all the poor come and take the leavings. If a newly married couple comes to one of these feasts, they have to bow before each of their ancestors and ask their blessing "for love and harmony, and for many children."

The remembrance of the dead also continues at home. Some women make sure to leave food on the table, convinced that the dead come by at night. After starving all winter, the dead need to eat as well. "If you don't feed your departed parents over Radonista," it is said in the villages, "then no one will remember you when you die."

CHAPTER 21
BRIGHT WEEK

The first week of Easter is like an extended single day of feasting. Joyful and bright. According to a pious folk tradition, the sun only set eight days after Christ's resurrection. So it's no surprise that the Russian folk called the week after Easter "Bright Week."

In pre-Revolutionary Russia, the bells rang almost without stopping for an entire week. Bread, the symbol of life, was blessed with a special prayer on Bright Saturday and kept for the use of the sick during the whole year.

The doors leading to the sanctuary, usually closed, revealed all the mystical happenings of the liturgy. These opened gates symbolized the destruction of the doors of hell and the opening of the gates to Paradise. With the Resurrection of the Son of God who destroyed physical death, every person now can walk the way to eternal life.

Folk traditions connected this week with various rites of spring's rebirth and the renewal of life.

A universal sense of joy pierced through all the festal days, and after liturgy people continued to express their joy in open air festivals.

THE PARADE OF THE BRIDES

This week's celebrations also used to have marriage connotations. In the Ryazan region, young women of marriageable age gathered on the main square of every village, in front of the church, for a special parade

Those who wanted to take part in the parade flaunted their beauty for the benefit of the village. Afterwards, they rode through the village on horses. During this process, the matchmakers presented them formally to every man they passed.

In the Archangelsk region, the girls dressed up in their finest and gathered in a public place to play the *bacha*. This was a long, painted stick. They used the stick to knock down figurines placed on the ground. This was a very popular event, and many people gathered to cheer on the girls.

HOLLERING AT THE YOUNG COUPLES

Young men bedecked themselves in their finest as well to take part in the rite of "hollering at the young couples." These were any couples that got married since last Pascha. The men began by passing through the courtyards in their own villages, but then they'd travel on to neighboring ones as well.

The songs they'd sing (at the top of their lungs) included congratulations for the young couples. Some songs were filled with useful advice for the young wife to help her get used to her new family.

Often, the songs included lists of actions for a wife to please her husband, his mother and father, and the rest of his family. Usually, after the "hollering," which included the names of all the visitors, all the young families concluded the festivities by visiting each other's houses for the rest of the week.

PASSING INTO A NEW SOCIAL STATUS

On Bright Week in many regions, newly married couples took part in rites that strengthened their new status as married people. In the Vladimir region, young couples visited the houses of older married women. They brought gifts of pies and eggs, a kind of admission fee into the society of married people.

In Kostroma, however, the older married women came to the homes of newly married couples, with ritual demands that the wife would let them in.

The young bride opened the door with these words. "My dear neighbors, my dear doves, love me and care for me, take me in as one of your new friends." Then, everyone sat down for the festal meal.

Everyone visited everyone on Bright Week. But all the feasting was always done properly and with dignity, without the usual excess. The village streets were always filled with people walking about, singing, dancing, playing games, doing figures while singing. Some people came out to show off with their best clothes, others showed their children off.

PILGRIM SONGS

Wandering pilgrims had an entire genre of songs to choose from. Pilgrims were usually men, walking from yard to yard. After wandering pilgrims largely became a thing of the past, the young men of the village played the part of the pilgrim.

In some villages, there were strict times for "pilgrim songs". Children could sing them in the morning, youths at noon. After lunch, it was the women. The men sang them closer to the evening.

Eventually, this became something like caroling on Christmas. A leader of the choir—a "precentor" or "intoner"—chose the songs and collected the caroling gifts. Every home expected the coming of the "pilgrim choir." It was considered good luck.

WALKING ABOUT

From the beginning of Bright Week, the youth began their spring open-air parties. The places for these parties were strictly chosen—only the central square or a green meadow next to a river.

An indispensable part of these parties was swinging on swings. This goes back to deep pagan antiquity, when people thought that swinging on swings helped the crops grow faster.

CHAPTER 22
WHY DO SOME ICONS DEPICT BATTLES?

I n a recent article in the Russian magazine *Foma*, the artist Dmitrii Trophimov asked an interesting question. Why do some icons depict battle scenes?

The answer is in some ways unexpected.

Battle scenes, more often than not, appear not in icons, but in miniature illuminations in the margins of manuscripts. When they do appear in proper icons, there's usually a good reason for it. Perhaps the most famous "war-like" icon is the so-called "Battle of the Novgorodians with the Suzdalians."

This icon depicts a miraculous deliverance of Novgorod by the icon of the Mother of God of the Sign in 1170. This was right in the middle of the tense period sometimes called the Internecine Wars, a time when rival cities battled each other for power almost constantly (and a time period I recreate in my third novel, The Heart of the World). The army of Suzdal had besieged Novgorod. It got so bad that the Suzdalians had already decided which streets of the city would be destroyed in which order.

At that time, the icon of the Mother of God (later called "the Icon of the Sign") was brought into the stockade as part of a liturgical procession. As it processed, the arrows of the Suzdalians began to pierce the icon, and the image began to shed real tears. As soon as that happened, a storm descended out of nowhere so quickly, it terrified the Suzdalians. In the confused murk, they began to shoot at each other and were eventually routed by the army of Novgorod.

Another popular theme for such military icons is the Battle on the Neva of St. Alexander Nevsky. However, this scene is usually not the main image, but a side panel or a background motif. The battle of Kulikovo Field can also be seen in some icons as a background motif.

Even though actual bloodshed isn't shown on the icon, the drama of battle is given stylized life. Armed warriors are gathered together like a monolith or like a balled fist. Spears bristle upward. To show the massive size of battle, iconographers used this kind of "shorthand"—a few horses to indicate the the whole host, a bunch of shields above them, and above the shields— many helms and spears. The retreating army is in tattered disarray in marked contrast to the monolith of the army of the victorious.

In such icons, most of the faces are not particularly recognizable. In icons of the battle of Kulikovo Field (the first significant military victory of the Rus against the invading Mongols), we can recognize St. Dmitrii Donskoy and the two warrior-monks Peresvet and Osliabia. In the icon of the victory over Suzdal, the Novgorodian army is led by none other than Sts. Boris and Gleb, Great-martyr George, and Great-martyr Dmitrii, who are all paragons of military virtue (though for different reasons).

As for the icon of St. Alexander Nevsky battling the invading Crusaders, the armies of heaven themselves step into battle on Prince Alexander's side. Interestingly, both the "good guys" and the "bad guys" are painted with the same neutral expressions.

So ultimately the answer to the question is that battles are painted on icons when the events had not merely historical but spiritual significance as well. The battle in such cases is connected with a labor for the sake of the faith and is always won with God's direct aid or by the prayer of His mother, and often with the military support of the angels and the saints.

CHAPTER 23
HOW ICONOGRAPHERS DRAW
THE SOUL

I n my third novel (*The Heart of the World*), one of the characters is given a choice–to remain inside a broken body, or to allow the soul to take flight. The character chooses to fly away in the form of an eagle.

This choice is not accidental. When poets wonder about the wandering of a soul after death, they like to compare it with a butterfly, a six-winged angel, or a bird. The same is true of iconographic symbolism of the soul.

The soul's immateriality is most often depicted by drawing it as a bird in flight. The eagle symbolizes the bravery of the flying spirit, the swan symbolizes its purity, but the most often used visual symbol was the white dove. It's a kind of "echo" of the Spirit-dove in the Gospel account of Christ's baptism.

THE SOUL AS CHILD

This iconographic symbol reveals the primordial purity of the soul that was lost in the Fall. This purity is increasingly lost as a person wallows in sin more and more over the course of his lifetime. The most obvious example of this iconographic motif is Christ holding the soul of His mother in the form of a child.

This is significant, because Orthodox theology makes it clear that Mary was the only human being to not willingly commit a sin.

We also see the depiction of the human souls in general as a child.

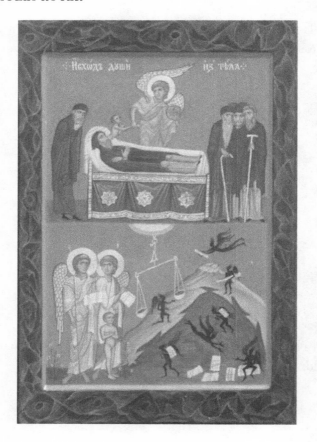

In some icons of the final judgment, there is a section called "the souls of the righteous are in the hand of God." In it, the divine hand holds the souls of the saints (in the forms of children). Around them, angels and demons fight over the rest of humanity, while the saints are protected.

THE SOUL AS A BRIDE

Russian wood-printers of the 18th century came up with an original allegory of the soul. The pure soul, as expressed from a poem of that time, is like "a bedecked bride, brighter than the sun, and the moon is under her feet, while on her head is a royal crown."

This icon is a literal illustration of that poem:

The elegant bride wears a crown. She has a nimbus (purity) and wings, which symbolize her righteous life.

The sun and moon are widely-used symbols of Christ and the Mother of God, respectively.

There are other, no less cryptic, symbols in this painting. The soul holds a pitcher, from which it pours tears of repentance. Thereby, it extinguishes the fire of sinful passions and even casts down the devil himself. She also holds a lion, the symbol of sins that are tamed by prayer and fasting. Here we also see a humbled serpent.

Two more interesting details. In her hands she holds a fruitful tree—the eternal symbol of life. The naked body sitting in the dark room is symbolic of a sinful soul. It serves as a striking anti-mirror image of the pure soul, reminding the viewer that both fates are possible for each human soul.

CHAPTER 24

WHY RUSSIANS INSIST ON CALLING RUSSIA "HOLY"

A reader of my first attempt at writing a novel noticed that I seemed to be obsessed with the idea of American exceptionalism. He was only partially right.

I'm not a fan of American exceptionalism (look where it's gotten us, after all). I am, however, a fan of Russian exceptionalism. Now, before you dismiss that outright, it might be useful to consider the history of that strange, elusive idea known as "Holy Russia."

WHAT IS HOLY RUSSIA?

The Russian word for "holy" (*sviatoi*) is etymologically connected with the word "bright." Both words are ancient, and the root of both goes back to an Indo-European antiquity. In other languages, there are similar words that mean "light," or "world," or "day," as well as something white, pure, shining.

The contemporary Russian philosopher and cultural historian Valery Lepakhin notes that in old Russian epic poetry "Holy Rus" is equated with "the white (or wide) world" and "Mother Earth." Take, for example, the call to arms of the most famous bogatyr from the epic poetry, Ilya Muromets:

And then his agile feet walked,
His white hands worked,
And he saw the wide, white world."

Dobrynia Nikitich (the second most famous of the "three warriors," says this about himself:

" I would no longer ride, not I, through Holy Rus.

And he is also described thus:

He was an exceptionally brave warrior,
A mighty warrior of Holy Rus!"

The "Song of the Fall of the Russian Land" (13th century) begins with the following words:

" O, how brilliantly bright and beautifully adorned is the land of Rus!"

In the "Poem about the Book of the Mysteries," (Golubi-naia Kniga), we read these words:

Holy Rus is a land that is mother to all lands,
Apostolic churches are built on her.
They pray to the crucified God,
To Christ Himself, the King of Heaven.
Therefore, holy-Rus-land is mother to all lands.

∾

INTERESTINGLY, THE WORD "RUS" IS ALSO etymologically similar to the word "light." After all, even contemporary Russian has preserved the old word "rusy" (light-haired). In 911, the Rus ("rusy") signed a treaty with Byzantium. The language of the treaty calls Prince Oleg "His Brightness." An Arab chronicler of the tenth century, Ahman ibn Fadlan, in an otherwise unflattering portrayal of the Rus, mentions that one of their rulers had the title "bright prince."

This association of "Russian" with "bright" remained inherent in the Russian language for a long time. Both Russians and Europeans called the Kingdom of Muscovy "White Russia." Foreigners continued to use this term until the beginning of the 18th century. You can even find it on some European maps.

"The White Tsar" is praised often in Russian folk songs. Other European names for the Russian Tsar included "illustrissimus" (most illustrious, or bright) or even "albus" (white). From the 16th century on, he was called "the White Tsar" in the East as well. Tibetan monks named Nicholas II "the White Tsar." (They believed he was a bodhisattva of the White Tara.)

HOLINESS AS RESPONSIBILITY

At the same time, by the 16th century, "Holy Russia" as a term began to acquire a distinctly religious connotation, much of which was tied up with apocalyptic fears concerning the 7,000th year after creation (1492). Elder Filofei, in his famous letter, wrote to Tsar Vasilli III as "the all-bright and highly-enthroned lord, the Grand Christian Prince who shines brightly in Orthodoxy, the lord of all, the rein-holder of all holy and great Russia."

The elder reminded the Grand Prince that after the fall of the first and second Rome, only the Russian Church "shines in its Orthodox Christian faith over the entire firmament more brightly than the sun." He then insisted:

 Let Your Mightiness know this: all Orthodox

Christian kingdoms have united under a single ruler, and you alone under the heavens are known as the all-holy and pious Tsar."

The elder, for the first time, insisted on Russia's high calling, and on the responsibility of its rulers to uphold that calling.

After this usage, "Holy Russia" stopped being an ethnic indicator. It's not by accident that Prince Andrei Kurbskii, in his letters to Ivan the Terrible, spoke of the Russian state as "The Holy Russian Empire." In the 17th century, the historical epic "The Tale of the Siege of Azov" recalled the times of the epic heroes, the "bogatyrs of Holy Rus." But now, the bogatyrs have obtained an explicitly religious significance:

> Now we, miserable ones, part with your holy icons, with the Christians and all Orthodox. Never again will we step on Holy Rus! Death has come to us, sinners, in the desert. All for the sake of your miraculous icons, for the faith of Christ and the name of the Tsar, the entire Tsardom of Muscovy!

In the beginning of the 19th century, the idea of "Holy Rus" had a second wind. With the patriotic fervor of the Napoleonic Wars, the old Russian epics were reprinted for the first time in centuries. The historian Nikolai Karamzin was the first to call his homeland "Holy Russia." Naturally, this usage was intended as the most exalted possible praise. Pushkin himself wrote, "O Holy Rus! My Fatherland! I am yours!"

And this wasn't necessarily a religious title any longer. For example, an official manifesto of Emperor Nicholas I, published after the French Revolution of 1848, had the following words:

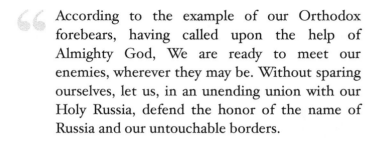 According to the example of our Orthodox forebears, having called upon the help of Almighty God, We are ready to meet our enemies, wherever they may be. Without sparing ourselves, let us, in an unending union with our Holy Russia, defend the honor of the name of Russia and our untouchable borders.

Holy Russia, be Holy!

The poet Prince Peter Vyazemsky reacted to the language of the manifesto of Nicholas I in a poem titled "Holy Russia." Though he was a free-thinking radical in his youth, he was able to beautifully express the heavy responsibility of the calling of "Holy Russia." In other words, Russia must strive to be holy in deed, not just in word.

Zhukovsky, another great poet, wrote a letter to Vyazemsky, in which he expressed his hope that the title of Holy Russia will never lose its profound meaning, even if it becomes commonplace. Here are his astounding words:

In the expression 'Holy Russia' you can hear the entirety of our unique history...It received its profound meaning from the times that we were divided...when there were many small princedoms dependent on the Grand Princedom. When we all united, it was not to become Russia, but Rus, that is, not a government, but a family. We all had a single fatherland, a single faith, a single tongue, the same remembrances and traditions. This is why, even in the bloodiest Internecine Wars, when Russia still did not exist, when the princes constantly fought each other for power, there was still a single, living, undivided Holy Rus for all.

In the 1850's, Vyazemsky developed his thought concerning Holy Russia even further in his so-called "Prayerful Thoughts":

Heaven forbid that in the darkness and vanity of life,
We will grow proud as Pharisees,
Puffed up in our own holiness, rebuking others,
Forgetting that pride is a great sin.
Not for glory, not for honor, did the tablets of the
   nation
Give our Russia the name "holy."
But to caution us, to remind us, as a testament.
We must preserve from our earliest years
The fear of God, and love, and the pure fire of faith.
So that our good deeds and good examples,
Bequeathed to us in ancient simplicity,
We may pass on to our sons in full.

So by the 19th century, "Holy Russia" had two meanings.

- A name for Russia as a whole, as in the epic poems
- The "mystical ideal of Russia" as a haven for a "new chosen people"

HOLY RUSSIA TODAY

This second meaning of "Holy Russia" is the one most commonly encountered in church hymnography. It was included for the first time in the service composed for the canonization of Patriarch Germogen, right before the Revolution of 1917:

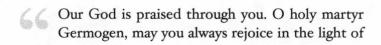

Our God is praised through you. O holy martyr Germogen, may you always rejoice in the light of

His countenance and constantly pray that Holy Russia will not fall.

The service to all Russian saints (composed in 1918), has perhaps the most famous usage of this phrase:

 O Holy Russia! Preserve the Orthodox Faith!

The service was confirmed by the Council of 1918. That year, "Holy Russia" was only beginning its historical trials, the worst of its history. The communists themselves understood that they were toppling not merely Russia, but "Holy Russia." See this excerpt from "The Twelve" by Blok:

> *"Comrade, hold on to your gun, be brave!*
> *Let's put a bullet into Holy Russia –*
> *Into ancient, sturdy,*
> *wood-hutted,*
> *Fat-assed Russia!*
> *Yeah, yeah, without the cross!"*
> *(translated by Maria Carlson)*

IT WAS INTO THIS WORLD OF COMMUNISM VS AN IDEALIZED Holy Russia that I was born. All the stories I heard in childhood were about it. My first identity crisis as a teenager was connected with it. Not surprisingly, the themes of identity and the idea of the "election of a nation" are central to my novel *The Song of the Sirin*. I still wonder about it—what is Holy Russia, really? Can it still exist, even in today's broken version of the land I love?

I hope so.

CHAPTER 25
CITATIONS

T he following articles and books were consulted in the translation and writing of this book

≈

Windows: https://cyrillitsa.ru/actual/567-okno.html

≈

Cradle: https://cyrillitsa.ru/past/21608-lyulka.html

≈

Ritual   Lamentation: https://russian7.ru/post/51196/full/

≈

Marriages in Old Russia: https://russian7.ru/post/svdb/

≈

BEHAVIORAL CONVENTIONS IN OLD RUSSIA: HTTPS://
russian7.ru/post/bonton/

∾

MYTHS OF RUSSIAN CUISINE: HTTPS://RUSSIAN7.RU/POST/5-
zabluzhdenijj-o-russkojj-kukhne/full/

∾

LOST IN TRANSLATION: HTTPS://ARZAMAS.ACADEMY/
materials/430

∾

BIZARRE RUSSIAN SAYINGS: HTTP://WWW.FRESHER.RU/2016/
07/05/russkie-krylatye-frazy-tajnyj-smysl/#

∾

RUSSIAN ROSETTA STONE: HTTPS://FOMA.RU/POCHEMU-
berestyanyie-gramotyi-stali-sensatsiey.html

∾

KIEVAN RUS FACTS: HTTPS://RUSSIAN7.RU/POST/SAMYE-
neozhidannye-fakty-o-kievskoy-ru/full/

∾

NAMING CONVENTIONS FOR PRINCES: HTTPS://ARZAMAS.
academy/materials/713

∾

MEDIEVAL MOSCOW:
https://ru.wikisource.org/wiki/
Народная_Русь_(Коринфский),   https://foma.ru/5-
udivitelnyih-faktov-ot-srednevekovogo-moskvoveda.html

≈

RADONITSA, BRIGHT WEEK, MASLENITSA, RUSSIAN SPRING,
The Meeting of the Lord: https://ru.wikisource.org/wiki/
Народная_Русь_(Коринфский)

≈

ICONIC BATTLE SCENES:
https://foma.ru/pochemu-na-ikonah-izobrazhayut-
srazheniya.html

≈

ICONOGRAPHY OF THE SOUL: HTTP://FUND.CYRILLITSA.RU/
pravoslavie/4754-ikonografiya-dush.html

≈

HOLY   RUSSIA: HTTP://WWW.NSAD.RU/ARTICLES/CHTO-
znachit-svyataya-rus

ALSO BY NICHOLAS KOTAR

The Song of the Sirin
The Curse of the Raven
The Heart of the World
The Forge of the Covenant
How to Survive a Russian Fairy Tale
Heroes for All Times

ABOUT THE AUTHOR

Nicholas Kotar is a writer of epic fantasy inspired by Russian fairy tales, a freelance translator from Russian to English, the resident conductor of the men's choir at a Russian monastery in the middle of nowhere, and a semi-professional vocalist. His one great regret in life is that he was not born in the nineteenth century in St. Petersburg, but he is doing everything he can to remedy that error.

CPSIA information can be obtained
at www.ICGtesting.com
Printed in the USA
JSHW081126210723
45153JS00003B/229